MOVIES AND THE MORAL ADVENTURE OF LIFE

MOVIES AND THE MORAL ADVENTURE OF LIFE

Alan A. Stone

Foreword by Joshua Cohen

A Boston Review Book

THE MIT PRESS Cambridge, Mass. London, England

MIT Press books may be purchased at special quantity
discounts for business or sales promotional use. For
information, please e-mail special_sales@mitpress.mit.edu or
write to Special Sales Department, The MIT Press,
55 Hayward Street, Cambridge, MA 02142.

This book was set in Adobe Garamond by *Boston Review*
and was printed and bound in the United States of America.

Designed by Joshua J. Friedman

Library of Congress Cataloging-in-Publication Data
Stone, Alan A.
  Movies and the moral adventure of life / Alan A. Stone ;
  foreword by Joshua Cohen.
      p.   cm. — (Boston Review books)
  ISBN: 978-0-262-19567-6 (hardcover : alk. paper)
  1. Motion pictures—Moral and ethical aspects. I. Title.
PN1995.5.S75 2007
791.43—dc22   2007013762

10   9   8   7   6   5   4   3   2   1

For Karen, Douglas, and David

CONTENTS

Joshua Cohen

FOREWORD

ALAN STONE IS A HUMANIST, AND IN these essays he writes about the exploration of human life in film—the great modern, democratic medium for reflection on our individual and collective lives.

Stone writes about art films and blockbusters, domestic and foreign, and he commands an extraordinary range of historical, literary, cultural, and scientific reference. His intellectual scope reflects his unusual personal history: professor of law and medicine, football player at Harvard in the late 1940s, director of medical training at McLean Hospital in the mid-1960s, and adviser to the Justice Department in the aftermath of the Waco disaster (he was a highly critical member of the behaviorial-science panel evaluating the government's action). Stone was also a Freudian analyst who broke from the analytic tradition in a much-discussed 1995 keynote address to the American Academy of Psychoanalysis. Arguing that "psychoanalysis and Freud belong to the arts and humanities," he said that analysis would live on not as science, but as reflection on what he called *the moral adventure of life*. Pursuing that reflection, Stone turned his attention to film.

Alan Stone's interest in film focuses principally on message rather than medium. For him, films are texts, and he is engaged more by their ideas than by their visual presentation, more by their content than by the mode of their production, more by their power to move us (and some of us more than others) than by their commercial success. To be sure, issues about pressures to commercial success inevitably loom large in discussions of contemporary movies. But while Stone sometimes expresses skepticism about the aesthetic effects of such pressures, he also understands their potential moral significance. There is, he agrees, something particularly admirable about the achievement of a great director who risks a reputation and successfully brings a large idea to a broad audience. Thus, Stone can write of *Schindler's List* that Steven Spielberg's "accomplishment cannot be gainsaid. He is vindicated both as a director and a Jew. He made his kind of film, a film that makes the Holocaust a part of popular culture; by celebrating the few who survived, Spielberg has put unforgettable human faces on the nameless dead."

I said that Stone is a humanist: the large purpose of his essays is, by reflecting on film, to explore what it means to be human. Though predisposed to melodrama, films provide particularly compelling occasions for such exploration. Ronald Dworkin distinguishes the view that the value of a life lies in the quality or magnitude of its impact on the world—the good that issues from it—from the view that its value lies in the quality of an agent's response to life's challenge. As the phrase "moral adventure" suggests, Stone is drawn to the latter view.

For Stone, responding to life's challenge begins in an honest appreciation of life's sheer complexity. It continues through an open-eyed recognition of the plenitude of human possibilities and a willingness—risking all—to live one of those possibilities with the heart's passion and mind's conviction. And it is shaped throughout by a grip on the reality of other people sufficiently strong to embrace love and resist the temptations to moral skepticism. Stone's essays pursue these themes by reflecting on characters in the films, the ambitions of directors, and the experience of audiences.

The importance of complexity in life's moral adventure comes through sharply in Stone's more critical essays. Consider his discussion of *Lolita*, Adrian Lyne's 1997 film version of Vladimir Nabokov's novel. Nabokov, Stone reminds us, detested Freud. *Lolita* was Nabokov's great attack on Freudian simplifications of life. By turning Humbert Humbert into a tragic pedophile, Lyne commits simplification through moralizing distortion. Roughly a third of Stone's reviews are about written texts "translated" into film, and issues of fidelity to the original often emerge in those reviews. But for Stone, a lack of fidelity in itself is not a deficiency: the sin of Lyne's *Lolita* is not that it differs from Nabokov's, but that it reduces life to manageable proportions.

But celebrating life's complexity is not enough. Stone's enthusiasms run particularly to films that enlarge our sense of human possibilities. Marleen Gorris's *Antonia's Line* gives us an emotionally vivid grip on a social world beyond patriarchy. In *Thirteen Conversations About One Thing*, the Sprecher sisters forcefully express the power of sheer contingency in human life, the frailty of our moral achievements, and the possibilities of redemption through the plainest human gestures. *American Beauty* reveals the place of beauty in ordinary human experience, shows how beauty draws us outside ourselves, but also reminds us that beauty and justice are distinct goods, with no intrinsic connection. *Un Coeur en Hiver* helps us to rediscover love, *The King of Masks* to restore our faith in human nature, and *Ma Vie en Rose* to experience an empathy beyond mere tolerance.

Alan Stone's essays are not, however, simply about complexities and enlarged possibilities: life is a *moral* adventure, and Stone's essay on *Thirteen Days* arguably makes the deepest moral point. Stone tells the story of his playing football at Harvard with Bobby Kennedy and Kenny O'Donnell. The young Bobby Kennedy, we are told, mixed ferociousness with a striking confidence in his own judgment and—himself "too small to play football"—a profound identification with the underdog. These qualities came together in the terrible 13 days in

1962 that nearly destroyed the world. Stone considers that his classmate Bobby Kennedy's "moral intuitions may have been a virtue in this crisis":

> In his mind, the United States picking on Cuba was like a big guy picking on a little guy. He was not prepared to give up moral convictions in the face of technical expertise. The best line in the film is given to JFK, but it also applies to Bobby: "There is something immoral about abandoning your own judgment."

Whatever the qualities of judgment that produced the crisis, Robert Kennedy's human instinct—not expertise, but a profound confidence and capacious decency—helped to save us all. No surprise that the film made Alan weep.

This is a large lesson about personal and political morality: a lesson about democracy, powerfully expressed in this supremely democratic medium, and passionately presented by Alan Stone as an essential experience in the moral adventure of his own life.

Joshua Cohen is the co-editor of Boston Review, *a professor of political science, philosophy, and law at Stanford University, and the director of the Program on Global Justice at Stanford's Freeman Spogli Institute for International Studies.*

MOVIES AND THE
MORAL ADVENTURE
OF LIFE

Believing in Love

Un Coeur en Hiver, 1992

UN COEUR EN HIVER, WRITTEN AND DI-
rected by Claude Sautet, is the negation of a
love story; and in our postmodern world, negation can have the deepest power of instruction. Not that this marvelous film is didactic
or ponderous. Like the fragile violins that the
protagonist, Stéphane, repairs, it is delicate and
beautifully crafted. It is an uncompromisingly
sophisticated work that never condescends to
its audience.

Sautet, an auteur, has joined a modern
psychological drama with a medieval morality play. All his characters except for Stéphane
are recognizable personalities; if we cannot pre-
dict their behavior, we can certainly under-

stand it after the fact. They all belong in the psychological drama, and many moviegoers will want to see this film as an old-fashioned study of character. But Stéphane's personality is an unsolvable mystery, and one cannot say about him that his psychology is his destiny. As Stéphane's character undercuts and challenges settled conventions of thought, Sautet takes us beyond determinist psychology and into the moral adventure of life.

Stéphane (Daniel Auteuil) and Maxime (André Dussollier) are partners in the violin business. They buy, sell, repair, and construct the finest stringed instruments for a carriage trade of musicians. Maxime—worldly, ingratiating, sensitive to the moods of others—has all the small talk that puts people at ease. He is the classic outside man: expansive, engaging, and expert at dealing with the temperamental artists who need to be reassured about their treasured instruments. Stéphane is the classic inside man: the master craftsman who can find and repair the slightest flaws because he fully understands the music as well as the instruments. He is enigmatic and socially insensitive, less than handsome but with an intriguing face that Sautet makes the most of through prolonged close-ups.

Stéphane's life is monachal. His immaculate button-down shirts are his clerical collar. Unmarried, he lives in rooms behind the shop, apparently desiring no pleasures beyond the satisfactions of work. He seems to have no need for other people and no dreams of love. Music is his only dream. The French, who can make waiting on tables a high art form, have more than any other people preserved the tradition of dignified artisanship. Stéphane, once a serious student violinist, is obviously a master craftsman. But only Sautet's French imagination would allow us to recognize and celebrate the heroic qualities of a man in his vocation.

Maxime, in contrast, is a sybarite who happily mixes business with the pleasures of the flesh. He is living the fast track: married, having affairs, traveling all over Europe, hobnobbing with concert artists. From the outset, it is clear that the partnership between these men is perfect.

THE FILM OPENS WITH THE METICULOUS Stéphane gluing the top of a violin in place. He utters Maxime's name. Maxime, needing no instruction, arrives from the front office at the correct moment to screw the wooden vises in place. The partners work together, play racquetball together, and seem to have an enviable friendship. But Stéphane does not appear to reciprocate Maxime's affection.

If home and family are the center of ordinary people's lives, Sautet's characters have no center. Many of the scenes in Sautet's movie take place in the same restaurant—their public place for private conversations. At such dinners in the past, Maxime had no compunction about describing his extramarital affairs to Stéphane. But this conversation is different. Something important has happened: he is in love. He has kept this affair secret, even from Stéphane, because he wanted to protect Camille (Emmanuelle Béart)—a beautiful and talented young concert violinist. Maxime has been touched by grace; he admires as well as loves Camille and has decided to leave his wife for her. Stéphane is less than gracious in his response to these revelations.

A standard psychoanalytic take on Stéphane's reaction might describe him as a jilted lover—a woman has come between two men who have a latent homosexual attachment. Sautet's screenplay permits such ideas to surface. Thus, Stéphane looks across the restaurant at Camille, who is sitting with her agent, the mannish Régine, and pointedly asks Maxime whether he has broken up a couple.

The relationship between Camille and Régine is another variation on the theme of nonreciprocal love that each of the relationships in this movie presents. Régine, the strong older woman, has taken Camille, the young artist, under her wing, cultivated her talent, promoted her career, and lovingly fed her ego. But the relationship that once nourished Camille now suffocates her. She wants to break out and assert her independence. But in Maxime she has found another older figure who will care for her in much the same parental way. It is a change without growth, and we soon see that it too is a non-reciprocal love that has not fully engaged her. If Stéphane's question about Camille and Régine was meant to provoke, Maxime quickly defuses the tension by insisting that Régine is the best friend of Camille's mother. Stéphane then presses Maxime about how his wife is dealing with this new turn of events. But Maxime refuses to be offended. With worldly wisdom he declares that in relationships someone always gets hurt.

If in relationships, too, someone always has the dominant hand, Maxime seems to have it over Stéphane. He wins their racquetball games and has dismissed Stéphane as a possible competitor in the game of love. But now Stéphane is no longer willing to take a back seat to Maxime. The beautiful Camille is a promising concert violinist, a high priestess in the temple of music where the monastic Stéphane worships. Indeed, each of the characters in this movie worships in that same temple where art is God and music is prayer. Maxime, in possessing Camille, has found a place closer to the altar, and, perhaps for the first time, the devout Stéphane envies the less virtuous man.

It would be wrong to say that he purposefully sets out to seduce Camille. Stéphane never acts with clear motives. In that he is like Camus's existential protagonist in *The Stranger* who kills for no reason. But the subtle Sautet stops far short of Camus. His hero, Stéphane, *has* reasons and motives to make this beautiful woman love him, to reject her, and to suffer for his behavior. They just do not seem sufficient to explain his actions, and, in that insufficiency, Sautet creates the moral space that gives his fragile movie its profundity.

CAMILLE, AS IT TURNS OUT, STUDIED AS A child with the same violin teacher as both Maxime and Stéphane. The main characters gather at the teacher's home for a dinner party, and we see another non-reciprocal relationship: the elderly teacher's middle-aged companion turns out to be his cook and nurse but not his wife. Stéphane will overhear their desperate quarrels. (There is another musical metaphor here, with the theme of couples overheard quarreling played out again and again in variations among the major and minor characters.)

The teacher is the one person whom Stéphane seems to admire. He is a man of intellect, faithful to the church of music and exacting in his judgment. The teacher describes to Stéphane the young Camille, a girl he knew as hard and smooth, with a considerable temperament behind the hardness. No longer a student, Camille is at a critical moment in her career. She is preparing to record a sonata and trio by Ravel. Though her technical excellence is not in doubt, Camille has a chance to prove that she can achieve artistry.

When Maxime brings Camille to the shop so that Stéphane can find and fix the flaw in her violin, it is impossible not to sense the instant electricity between Stéphane and Camille. She is intrigued by his intensity, his exacting standards, his emotional unavailability. He fixes her instrument and then attends her rehearsal to listen. His presence seems to disturb her concentration. He leaves but returns later, and with a subtle adjustment the master craftsman further improves the violin's tone. Camille is soon dependent on him. Stéphane has become the mechanical and spiritual catalyst for her artistry. Having made himself necessary, he absents himself—and she is hooked, like a woman who falls in love with her psychiatrist.

She needs him, loves him, must have him. We begin to glimpse the temperament that will boil over in the scenes to come. Sautet's refined taste and subtlety are present everywhere in this movie, and it surely was inspiration to cast Auteuil and Béart, husband and wife, in the roles of Stéphane and Camille.

Camille reveals her love for Stéphane to Maxime, who, though incredulous, remains a man of the world in the best sense. He is prepared to step aside, at least temporarily. Indeed, knowing Camille's intense feelings, he asks Stéphane to attend the Ravel recording. Camille, inspired by her passion and believing it to be fully reciprocated by Stéphane, plays Ravel's ecstatic music as never before; it is a triumph. Filled with confidence, Camille wants to consummate her love. But in her moment of glory, when she surrenders herself body and soul to Stéphane, he refuses her.

The desolate Camille goes on a drunken binge and the next day confronts Stéphane in one of Sautet's restaurant scenes. There she explodes in a public display. After shaming herself and humiliating Stéphane, she leaves the restaurant. Maxime replaces her, and, standing over Stéphane like an outraged husband, slaps him in the face and sends him crashing to the floor. Auteuil plays the perfect bewildered victim—and the situation *is* slightly bewildering. After all, Maxime is furious with Stéphane because he did not sleep with the woman Maxime loves—and, of course, under the circumstances Maxime is right.

Stéphane's rejection of Camille ends his partnership with Maxime. His other woman friend who has been his only companion announces that she has found a man who cares for her. Stéphane goes on with his vocation, but he is almost alone in the world.

FOR MANY PEOPLE, LOVE HOLDS THE ONLY promise of transcendence. And romantic—yes, sexual—love is the closest most of us come to realizing the fulfillment of that promise. So when Stéphane rejects Camille's offer of love, Sautet surprises and defeats our expectations. The knee-jerk psychological reaction is to think that Stéphane must be crazy. In our dismay we deny his sanity. But in the morality play to which he belongs, his mysterious negation of love can illuminate our own hopes and fears as would-be lovers.

Why does he do it? Stéphane does not refuse out of loyalty to his friend Maxime. He had told Camille in an earlier conversation that Maxime was not his friend—only his partner. Nor does the refusal grow out of his love for some other woman, as Camille imagines. He has given his only woman friend no promise of love. Deep in their heart of hearts some people wonder if they are even capable of love. Stéphane might be one of them. Does he understand what has happened?

Stéphane openly acknowledges all of his possible neurotic motives to Camille—from sexual hang-ups to deviousness—but only to demonstrate that they are insufficient. He goes to the wise teacher, who raises other more existential reasons—from a need to demystify love to feelings of inadequacy. But those, too, are insufficient, and the teacher and his former student do not solve the mystery. In the end, neither Stéphane's character nor the web of relationships in which he and Camille are involved fully explain his refusal of this proud and beautiful woman. He refuses Camille because he does not believe in love. He is a man of rectitude, but without faith.

By refusing a complete psychological explanation, Sautet has left open for us the possibility of moral choice and lost opportunity: Stéphane has lost an opportunity in the moral adventure of his life—and one that we are made to feel may have been his best and only chance. In doing so, *Un Coeur en Hiver* raises questions about how the rest of us make our choices in the moral adventure of our lives.

EARLY IN THE MOVIE SAUTET SHOWS US that Stéphane's relationship with his teacher is of great significance to him—a son's admiring love for the ideal father. Toward the end of the film Stéphane is called back to the teacher's country home. The man is dying a painful death. Neither the woman who cares for him nor Maxime, who has already arrived, has the will to put him out of his misery. Stéphane, the man without sentiments, does what is necessary. The dying man looks at Stéphane and then looks to the bedside table where the medications are. Stéphane, the ultimate craftsman, approaches the task at hand and completes it with the practiced skill of a surgeon.

One might think that this death scene—a Dr. Kevorkian moment—is gratuitous, not really connected to the central dynamic of the film. It is also quite implausible that Stéphane would be adept with an intravenous syringe. Yet thematically, it ties everything together. The death of a loved one reminds us of our mortality, of missed opportunities for the expression of love, of what is most precious in life. In Stéphane's decisive action, we see the power of a will unmoved by sentiment. Immanuel Kant thought that passion was a disease of reason, but Sautet shows us through Stéphane that the absence of passion is a disease of human nature.

The final question that Sautet asks is whether Stéphane has been changed by these experiences. The answer is so subtle that it took this reviewer two viewings of the movie to catch it. The last scene, a coda, fittingly shows Stéphane sitting in a restaurant talking with Maxime. Camille arrives, and Maxime goes to get the car—they are a couple again. Briefly alone with Stéphane, Camille asks him about his feelings for the dead man. Stéphane's reply, wonderfully nuanced and appropriate to the delicate but rich tones of the film, is that he used to think the teacher was the only person he loved. I take it he now realizes that he loved

Camille and that he loved his friend Maxime as well. Camille tenderly kisses him goodbye and drives off with Maxime. She knows that the miraculous moment is irretrievably lost. Stéphane sits alone, a man who too late believes that love and music are part of the same dream. By negating love, Sautet has rediscovered its possibility.

Hollywood and Holocaust

Schindler's List, 1993

LIKE EVERY CHILD IN THE HUMAN FAMily, Stephen Spielberg still believes in miracles. And his underlying optimism and hope are a throwback not to Disney but to Frank Capra and Preston Sturges—the great happy-ending directors of Hollywood's past. In fact, movie nostalgia is one of Spielberg's trademarks. So when Spielberg decided to make a film about the Holocaust he took on a monumental task, and one not obviously suited to his talents. Furthermore, his personal Jewish identity was on the line. He knew he was making the most important film he had yet undertaken, and that anything less than a sweeping success would be a failure.

The Holocaust is the most important event in the history of world Jewry, and its memory is sacred to any Jew who acknowledges his Jewishness—sacred in all the complex and ambiguous ways of a fractious people. For almost three millennia, Jews of the diaspora have survived as an oppressed minority united in suffering—and not in political or military dominion. Still, no one can deny that the "chosen people" have prospered. And the modern world, overwhelmed by competing claims of victimhood, has grown weary of the Jew as the specialist in suffering and the Jewish dirges about *their* Holocaust. The non-Jewish world wants no more of the Holocaust, and for many Jews, including this writer, the subject seems too painful and too sacrosanct for Hollywood. Yet Spielberg met the challenge before him. He made *the* Hollywood movie about the Holocaust; a distinctive achievement that by its very terms—Hollywood and Holocaust—seems impossible.

Spielberg's achievement rests in large measure on the leap of creative imagination and faith it took to recognize that Thomas Keneally's novel *Schindler's List* would make a great movie. Oskar Schindler, the protagonist, is the non-Jew who mediates the Holocaust experience for the audience. Because he is a person with whom non-Jews can identify, he creates for them an emotional connection to the events of the film. And because of his otherness, he keeps Jews at a safe emotional distance from their own terror. For the non-Jews who do not really care about the Holocaust and for the Jews who care too much, he solves two basic psychological problems at once.

Moreover, since Schindler was a minor historical character, unknown to audiences, Spielberg and his actor, Liam Neeson, were free to create their own, larger-than-life Schindler. And like Schindler, the Irish actor Neeson was relatively unfamiliar to American film audiences and so did not carry the baggage of past roles into his part. Neeson's presence is iconic. His carved features and size suggest some Roman statue of a god come to life; he projects the magnetism and authority of the legendary film stars. Those qualities transform Oskar Schindler, failed businessman and bon vivant, into a mysterious and imposing personality who can carry the historical weight of the film.

When we first encounter Schindler, we see his back, his hands, his cache of money, and his preparations for a high-stakes gamble. We watch him bribe a headwaiter. Schindler is throwing his money around to ingratiate himself with Nazi authorities in the occupied Polish city of Kraków. We do not know exactly why he is doing it, only that he is a kind of magician, transforming the separate tables of a cabaret into one joyful drunken party of wine, women, and song for the Nazi officials. We learn that this is Schindler's only skill as a businessman; it allows him to set up shop as a war profiteer. He quickly establishes contact with Jewish operatives in the black market as well, so he can ply Nazi officials with luxury goods: they will grease the wheels for his business ventures.

Schindler clearly intends to exploit the situation, living as high as he can and packing away as much money as he can. He has followed the German army into occupied Poland like a carpetbagger, taking advantage of the war to exploit Jews, not to save them. He will be converted, but not like Saul, struck by revelation on the road to Damascus. Instead, as he watches the atrocities, a gradual process of self-discovery—which he does not himself understand—takes place. Jews beg for his help, which he eventually gives, spending his entire war profiteer's fortune and taking personal risks to do it.

How does this exploitative, high-living, self-indulgent man become the savior of so many Jews? Schindler's character—in the old-fashioned moral sense of the word—is the deepest mystery of this amazing story, and Spielberg and Neeson never really solve it. One possibility is that just as the real Schindler seized the easy opportunity to make money, he seized the easy opportunity to save Jewish lives—not because he was a hero or saint but because he was a man who could not resist opportunities and grand gestures. He takes over a wealthy Jew's lavish apartment just as he takes over a Jewish-owned factory. Like a child, he can deny himself nothing. Yet with his talents he manages to save more than a thousand Jews. As his gradual conversion begins in what may be the greatest human scene in this film, Schindler awakens from what the Holocaust poet-philosopher Elie Wiesel has called the greatest sin and punishment: indifference. The scene is convincing and believable because one sees the same convivial Schindler in this act of mercy.

It is a very hot day, and the Jews have been packed into cattle cars at the train station for transport to Auschwitz. The Nazis, joined by Schindler, are sipping cold drinks while their human cattle are dying of thirst and suffocation. Schindler, awakened by a moral sensibility, convinces an SS officer, Commandant Anon Goeth (Ralph Fiennes) to allow him to spray the desperate Jews with the fire hose. His futile gesture amuses the Nazis, who know how the train ride will end. But Schindler is saved from the sin of indifference.

Schindler might be the kind of man who is neither born to goodness nor achieves goodness but has goodness thrust upon him. In the moral adventure of life he simply finds himself in the right place at the right time to play the hero's part. The case of Schindler might then demonstrate that acts of good and evil are in large measure fortuitous, that saintliness is not required for great deeds, just as the case of the good German—the dutiful man who goes about killing Jews efficiently because that is his job—demonstrates that deeds of great evil are not confined to the wicked. Spielberg gives us many such good Germans, who chuck children under the chin and call old women "mother" before they slaughter them like cattle. Schindler is neither good nor evil. His sins are those of the flesh, and his virtues are those of the bon vivant who genuinely wants everyone to enjoy the party.

This postmodern view of Schindler as the opportunist who has goodness thrust upon him was certainly not Spielberg's intention. His own psychological interpretation of Schindler's conversion is ambiguous, though, and in the end so melodramatic that it is the major disappointment in the film's artful construction.

The character of Spielberg's Schindler evolves in a sequence of scenes in which he interacts with his accountant, Itzhak Stern (Ben Kingsley). Schindler knows that he is himself incompetent and that he needs Stern to run his enterprise. Stern recognizes Schindler for what he is: an opportunistic war profiteer. But as the world of Kraków's Jews collapses, Stern, a Jew himself, realizes that Schindler can be useful and becomes his faithful middleman, organizing and running the enterprise. The contrast between Stern's discipline and asceticism and Schindler's self-indulgence establishes both the characters.

At the same time, Schindler's indulgences contrast increasingly with the mad drunkenness and perverse violence of Commandant Goeth. But neither Stern nor Goeth are presented as rounded psychological characters. Stern has no private or personal life in the film. Although he has a family, his relationship to them is barely acknowledged. Above nepotism and all of the ugly, self-interested motives, he uses his position with Schindler to save people only on humanistic grounds: intellectuals, musicians, rabbis who are to be exterminated because they have no "essential skills." Stern is the "pure soul" of the film (no stretch for the actor who played Gandhi). Goeth is put together with smoke and mirrors. He is part sadistic madman, part fop, part alcoholic, and part fool. These parts do not make a believable commandant even in Hitler's camps. But both characters serve Spielberg's purpose: to establish a middle ground between good and evil for Schindler to occupy and within which he can move toward Stern and save his soul.

Yet Goeth's unreal character—uncontrollably cruel and taking pleasure in his cruelty—is on the screen for another reason, too. War has many horrors, but the most obscene is the sadism that pours from the hearts of so many human beings. Goeth is the human embodiment of those responsible for the Holocaust. He kills arbitrarily without rhyme or reason. He kills Jews who try to help, and he kills Jews who obstruct. He kills randomly for sport and systematically for policy. He kills with a long-range rifle, he kills with a pistol at point-blank range, and he kills without remorse. His is the modern figure of Satan in the guise of a psychotic sadist. Michel Foucault worried that madness had driven evil from the world, but Nazis like Goeth demonstrated that there is no moral distinction.

Surprisingly, Spielberg projected these archetypes of good and evil onto children as well. Children have been a characteristic presence in Spielberg's major films: *E.T.*, *Jaws*, *Close Encounters of the Third Kind*, the *Indiana Jones* series, and *Empire of the Sun*. Children powerfully evoke sympathetic identification and intense emotions. It is no surprise, then, that children figure in *Schindler's List*. Yet in a stroke of inspired balance, Spielberg has used them both as victimizers and victims. There is the memorable image of a young Polish girl screaming "Goodbye, Jews" in an ecstasy of hatred as her neighbors are taken away. And there is an even younger Polish boy making the universal, grisly gesture of the hand across the throat as the Jews pass in cattle cars toward Auschwitz. These children are Spielberg's reproach against those who say "We didn't hate Jews" and "No one knew." As counterpoint, there is the searing image of the Jewish boy in the labor camp desperately trying to find a hiding place to escape the ovens. His last resort is the latrine under the toilet holes. As the young boy jumps in we see other children we recognize from earlier scenes already hiding in the fecal sewage.

The horror of this image of children submerged in human waste is tolerable only because of Spielberg's decision to use black and white rather than color. So, too, we are spared the redness of the gushing blood in the many scenes in which Jews are shot point-blank through the head. Indeed, Spielberg's brilliant decision to film *Schindler's List* in black and white is a key ingredient in the movie's aesthetic success. Color intensifies most of the emotional values in film—as though part of our primitive brain were turned on by color information. Certainly this is true for images of sex and violence, both of which are portrayed in the film—but shot in black and white, they are less arousing to our basic instincts. The lack of color allows Spielberg to be explicit without becoming tastelessly graphic.

Spielberg's black and white also achieves aesthetic objectives. It echoes newsreels and documentaries of the Holocaust made at the time, thus establishing historical context and a feeling of authenticity. Yet the film doesn't completely lack color. At one point a Jewish mother and her daughter cross the screen, and the little girl is wearing a red coat. The signifier quickly vanishes until the film's most ghoulish scene. The Nazis are ordered to dig up all the Jewish corpses they have buried to incinerate the evidence of the slaughter of the Kraków ghetto. As the decomposing corpses are trundled in wagons to the fires we catch again a glimpse of the red coat among the dead.

Spielberg also brackets the film with color: at the beginning, as we watch two candles burn out, and near the end, when a candle is lit and burns against the darkness. Both times, in the white flicker of the flame we see the reddish-orange glow of combustion—the sign of life, extinguished and then rekindled. There are other choreographed moments that indicate how thoughtfully the film was edited.

Spielberg also makes good use of Kraków. The surviving gem of Poland's medieval cities, Kraków has a castle and cathedral that were spared by the armies that for centuries marched back and forth across the country. They are less than a half day's journey from the great rail crossings of Eastern Europe that meet at Auschwitz, chosen by the Germans as the most convenient location for their genocide. Anyone who has visited Auschwitz, as I have, will recognize how much the artifacts of the slaughter contribute to the images in the film. I walked around Auschwitz and wept as I saw heaps of children's shoes, gold dental fillings, eyeglasses, human hair, suitcases with Jewish names and addresses from all over Europe.

Spielberg has also filmed some of the most lurid scenes from high up and at a distance, reminiscent of Breughel's *Slaughter of the Innocents*, which, in the very act of affirming God's existence, denies His concern for us. But Spielberg's film is silent on the subject of God. His Jews go through the Holocaust without ever asking how God could do this to his chosen people. For those on his list Schindler is the only god in this film. His unexpected goodness is their miracle. He is the one who looks down from above at the Kraków slaughter. Perhaps conscious of the limits of his medium and the scope of his own talent, Spielberg leaves the problem of God to the rabbis. His film is not a philosophy of the Holocaust.

But if *Schindler's List* does not pose deep philosophical questions, it does provide some answers. Amon Goeth, the locomotives steaming into Auschwitz, the unrestrained hatred of the Poles, and the indifference of good Germans are all concrete answers to Hannah Arendt's abstract question of why so many Jews went unprotesting to their deaths. That Schindler saved so many Jews is also an answer to those who claimed nothing could be done.

Spielberg insists on confronting the explicit horror of the Holocaust, but not in a way that would drive the Jewish members of his audience out of the theater. Almost none of the Jewish characters we get to know well are killed. The children who hide in the latrine are saved. And even in the most terrifying moment, when the women and children on Schindler's list are mistakenly sent to Auschwitz, we are spared: hair cut and stripped naked they are herded into the showers. When water comes out of the first shower head, and then all the others, one weeps with relief, and we watch with them while the lines of other Jews, not on Schindler's list, are led toward the gas chambers. Spielberg's camera does not follow them to their destruction. Instead it pans to the ominous smoke and cinders blown from the chimney of the crematorium. We are expected to bear witness to the enormity of calculated genocide, but we are not required to watch it.

But having restrained the bathos for so long, Spielberg gives in to his worst impulses in the last few moments of the film. Schindler has not only taken heroic risks and spent most of his fortune to save his Jews and provide them sanctuary in his munitions factory in Czechoslovakia, he has also decided to manufacture only defective munitions and lose the rest of his money to sabotage the German war effort. When the war finally ends, the bankrupt Schindler delivers a marvelous speech convincing the guards to go home without killing his Jews. As though this were not enough, Spielberg adds a final scene in which Schindler has a convulsion of self-loathing as he berates himself for not saving more lives. His gold Nazi pin could have saved two lives, his automobile, five lives. He collapses in paroxysms of remorse, and his Jews step forward to take him in their arms and comfort him. In the background, we vaguely discern someone taking off his striped concentration-camp uniform and in Schindler's last scene he is wearing the inmate's garb. His transformation to heroic martyr is complete and utterly unbelievable. Yet this directorial lapse can be forgiven. Spielberg's risk-taking in the end is what saves *Schindler's List* from what it could have been—a film that merely manipulated filmgoers instead of leaving them in stunned silence as the final credits roll.

There will be some who find fault with Spielberg's movie, and particularly those who cringe at Schindler's last scenes. But Steven Spielberg's accomplishment cannot be gainsaid. He is vindicated both as a director and a Jew. He made his kind of film, a film that makes the Holocaust a part of popular culture; by celebrating the few who survived, Spielberg has put unforgettable human faces on the nameless dead.

A Second Nature

Antonia's Line, 1995

IN THE DUTCH FILMMAKER MARLEEN Gorris's first movie, *A Question of Silence* (1982), three women—strangers to each other—go berserk and kill the male proprietor of a dress shop whose sexism unleashes their repressed rage. Their lawyer later argues that they were not responsible, since they were victims of the centuries of humiliation and physical violation that have scarred the collective unconscious of every woman. This parable of justified rage put Gorris in the forefront of radical feminism, a position she consolidated with *Broken Mirrors* (1984), a savage depiction of male brutality to women that combined scenes from a brothel with scenes from the cellar of a serial killer, photographing a victim as she starves to death. Together, these man-hating jeremiads earned Gorris a reputation as "the apotheosis of angry militant Eurofeminism."

For nearly a decade, that reputation appeared to have been a marginalizing curse to the promising filmmaker. She disappeared into the Eurofeminist underground; and although she continued to work, her career as a creative writer and director seemed dead. But Gorris, though missing, was far from dead; by 1988 she had completed the screenplay for *Antonia's Line*, her astonishingly beautiful 1995 film that won the Oscar for Best Foreign Film. While her early films were guerrilla warfare—men were the enemy, and women took no prisoners—*Antonia's Line* imagines a truce in the gender wars. Drafted if not dictated by women, the terms of the truce grow from a simple premise: that women must create their own identity—that they are not to be defined, as Gorris has said, "through their roles as wife, mother, or daughter." Men can be accepted into this new world if they are willing to accept the matriarchal terms of the truce. *Antonia's Line* is about the new world—the lives, the families and the communities—created by that truce. What will it look like? How will women build families? How will they live, and how will they die?

Gorris calls her film "a fairy tale": an ironic comment on the possibility that women will actually achieve such independence, but also an accurate description of her aesthetic method. Transcending the bleak anger of her earlier films, Gorris has discovered in herself a sense of humor and used it to explore the whole gamut of human emotions. Every introspective human being knows that emotions come in unlikely mixtures and surprising oppositions: feelings of depression often lurk behind anger, tears unexpectedly accompany laughter. In its portrayals and provocations, *Antonia's Line* is a marvelous demonstration of the subtlety, complexity, and surprise of unfamiliar emotions.

Any film can play on an audience's emotions; that is Hollywood's specialty. Only a great film like *Antonia's Line* reveals a new way to live.

AS THE FILM OPENS, THE NARRATOR, WHO we will eventually discover is Antonia's great-granddaughter Sarah, matter-of-factly informs us that Antonia (Willeke Van Ammelrooy) knows even before she gets out of bed that this will be the last day of her life. There will be no explanation of how this knowledge came to her, why or how she will die. But this knowledge is presented neither as a frightening premonition nor as a step toward suicide. This simple, nuanced, and profound beginning sets the stage for an adult fairy tale about a world in which women have mysterious powers. Antonia will call her loved ones to her side; and Sarah, who is fascinated by death, will be given this precious opportunity to watch.

Antonia, weighed down but still handsome and unbowed by age, starts her last day with familiar morning routines: opening the shutters, feeding the goat. Then, as she looks out the kitchen window, her memory flashes back to the end of World War II; Antonia and her teenage daughter Danielle (Els Dottermans) are returning to the Dutch village where Antonia was born to claim the farm she has inherited. They enter the bedroom of her supposedly dead mother, who, it turns out, is still alive (though on her deathbed) and still cursing her unfaithful "shitbag" of a husband who died 30 years earlier. Her final words, after she recognizes Antonia, are "Late as usual." Antonia and her daughter are more curious and amused than sad. Gorris scripts and directs the mother's death scene for laughs, with the priest as the straight man.

When the dead mother suddenly sits up in her coffin during the funeral and bursts into "My Blue Heaven," we realize that this scene takes place only in the mind's eye of Danielle, whose creative fantasies add a note of magic realism to the film. In keeping with the mood and the affirmative feminine principle of the film, Danielle sees the tortured Christ on the cross—representing the male principle—turn his head and smile benevolently on the proceedings.

Running through *Antonia's Line* is a conflict between these two principles. According to the male principle—which rejects life as a source of unending misery, with death the only escape—man can suffer all his life because he is preoccupied with death and the search for meaning. In Gorris's vision, patriarchy is the main obstacle to human freedom, dignity, and fun. According to the life-affirming female principle, a child can thrive on her curiosity about death, and a woman can enjoy living because she does not expect life to reveal its secrets.

Gorris conveys these ideas in the development of the characters, who cannot be understood in "realistic" psychological terms, but instead as the incarnations of the two principles:

Antonia is the earth mother who absorbs and dispenses the not-so-simple wisdom of nature as she works her farm until she dies. She is the matriarch of a new line of women, and she accepts the cycle of life and death because she accepts nature in all its plenitude; her male counterpart, Crooked Finger (Mil Seghers), is a recluse with a house full of books and a mind crammed with learning, all apparently poisoned by melancholy. A tortured Schopenhauerian character who, having absorbed all the scientific male wisdom of Western civilization, is finally driven to suicide. No film in recent memory is at once so rich in ideas and so intellectually unpretentious. We are never forced to recognize the intellectual daring and craft of the filmmaker; we are carried along by the surprising flow of the narrative.

WE FIRST MEET ANTONIA'S DAUGHTER, Danielle, as a dark-haired, nondescript teenager in a shapeless dress. Her wish-fulfilling imagination at her grandmother's funeral pre-figures her talent. She will be an artist, and Antonia unpossessively sends her off to art school; bonds between women are important to Gorris, but they do not constitute identity. Danielle returns an artist but still unfulfilled. She wants a child, though like her mother she has no use for a husband. Antonia, who can solve any natural problem, takes her to the city and, by a happy mistake, to a home for unwed mothers. At the home they meet Letta, a hugely pregnant, vivacious woman who does not necessarily like getting pregnant or raising children, but loves being pregnant and giving birth. She is defined not by her role as wife or mother but by the fructified state of pregnancy. Delighted to help Antonia and Danielle fulfill their mission, she introduces Danielle to one of her male relatives.

Because of her passionate wish to be im-pregnated, Danielle is a demanding lover, and when the willing but finally exhausted young man falls asleep, we see Danielle standing on her head to help the sperm on its way. For the first time the camera reveals her shapely body. Back in her baggy dress she gaily runs from the hotel to join her mother and Letta, who have been waiting patiently. The women are conspiratorial and mischievous in their joy— the man has been used in this affair, though without mean spirit. We can believe he feels like Don Juan, not one of his victims. Having stood a naked woman and the conventional sexual escapade on their heads, Gorris has presented first death and now sex with dazzling ingenuity, thumbing her nose at patriarchal roles and the institutions that legitimize and delegitimize children.

Danielle gives birth to a girl, Thérèse, who is soon revealed to be an intellectual prodigy. When her schoolteacher Lara shows up to discuss this prodigy's education, Danielle takes one look at her—long-haired, blonde, and as unglamorous as Danielle—and it is love at first sight. Gorris presents their love with taste and judgment. The women are neither carefully platonic nor swooning—simply a young couple "naturally" falling in love with each other. Gorris knows that we cannot hold a mirror up to nature—that nature is itself a human invention; but *Antonia's Line* is her fairy tale, and this scene, and indeed the entire film, comes close to a convincing realization of naturalness. There is a feminist, perhaps lesbian agenda in this portrayal of love. But Gorris's art, with its reassuring good humor, transforms her political concerns into a moral project, lifting the film and Gorris's audience to a new acceptance and understanding of difference.

In this women-centered world, Crooked Finger is not the only man. Some have entered Antonia's world, and others, leftovers from the gender wars of *Broken Mirror*, lurk on it borders. There is one unforgiving example of patriarchy: a father matched by two brutal sons, a silenced wife, and a half-wit daughter Deedee.

Deedee is treated like an animal by the men in her family. When Danielle, who has gone to their farm to fetch a saw, catches the brother Pitte (Filip Peeters) raping Deedee, she picks up a pitchfork and throws it, skewering him just where you would expect. Pitte will disappear from the village wounded, though (unfortunately) not permanently incapacitated, with his hatred of women and his evil nature intact. Danielle takes Deedee to Antonia's farmhouse, where she is installed in a growing community. Antonia has already saved the village idiot Loony Lips (Jan Steen) from the torment of nasty little boys; and he has followed her faithfully thereafter. He and Deedee become a devoted couple. Antonia's dinner table further expands as the village priest moves in, soon to be joined by Letta of the pregnancy project. Recruited by Letta, the defrocked priest finally has a true calling—producing his own twelve apostles. In this allegory about the liberating power of nature, Gorris makes us value the eccentrics even as she spurns the patriarchal institutions that created them.

Antonia, the great matriarch, presides over her happy commune, enjoying the rhythms of the seasons and majestically sowing her seeds. But this handsome woman is not without male suitors, notably Bas (Jan Decleir), a widower with a string of obedient sons who follow him like ducklings. In yet another ingenious reversal of gender politics, Bas—a good and simple man—proposes to Antonia, explaining that his sons need a mother. Antonia tells him that she has no need for his sons. But if Antonia does not need a man, Bas seems to need Antonia. So farmer Bas and his obedient sons loyally attend Antonia, helping with the chores, until she finally tires of her self-imposed chastity. Prepared to offer Bas everything except her hand, she dictates terms: they are too old to impose their relationship on their families, and at their age once a week will be sufficient (though they agree to negotiate should a need for greater frequency arise). Bas builds a little hut in the countryside and, in a charming scene, carries Antonia over the threshold.

Soon lovemaking breaks out all over: the buxom, middle-aged Antonia, cavorting in the arms of her faithful Bas; Danielle and the schoolteacher; Deedee and Loony Lips, she a butterball and he a string bean stretched out over her; and Letta and her defrocked priest. The ardor of these couples grows until they are all making so much noise that the young prodigy, Danielle's daughter Thérèse, cannot sleep.

Into this Eden of innocent women and natural joy comes the serpent Pitte, who returns after many years to revenge himself on Danielle by raping Thérèse. While Deedee consoles Thérèse, Antonia takes up a rifle and tracks Pitte down in a bar. Unable to bring herself to kill him, she puts her curse on him; and in that awesome moment, one has no doubt that Antonia's curse carries the awful women's power the misogynist Dominican fathers feared when they wrote the *Malleus Maleficarum*. Pitte is cruelly beaten by the other young men, who discover what he has done. When he staggers home looking for help he is drowned by his own brother, who hates him and wants to inherit the family farm.

The narrator tells us that the proverb is not true: time does not heal all wounds. Thérèse has been forever scarred by the rape. In this Eden, rape is the primal sin, hardening the heart against love. Thérèse has been tutored by Crooked Finger, who, despite his bitterness, loves this girl and has shared his learning with her. She loves him, too—as daughters love fathers—in a relationship that Gorris allows to undercut the primary bonds between women that form the structure of *Antonia's Line*. Indeed, she is incapable of loving anyone but him. Letta's oldest son Simon has worshipped Thérèse from childhood, and although she does not love him, she gets pregnant by him and decides to have the baby—a girl, of course. But Thérèse has no maternal love for her child. She hands the newborn, Sarah, to Simon and turns back to her mathematics book. Simon, the father, will mother Antonia's great-grand-daughter.

As new life comes in Antonia's line, so comes death, sudden, surprising, but matter-of-fact and even humorous. But when Crooked Finger hangs himself it is quite a different matter. Gorris leaves us no emotional distance. Thérèse is heartbroken, and as Crooked Finger's body is cut down, little Sarah, peering through the window, takes in the whole catastrophe.

But one day as Antonia and Bas, now showing their age, get up from the dinner table to dance, we see that little Sarah has Danielle's gift. She imagines in her mind's eye that the dead have returned to life, and that Antonia and Bas are as young as when they first met. Antonia has already told us that life is the only dance we dance, but Gorris reassures us that

Antonia's line will go on dancing in her grand-daughter's creative mind. The earth mother, the painter, the intellectual prodigy, and the little student of death who tells the story: each has created a human identity. And that creativity is the hope of Antonia's line. However it comes out for them, Gorris has done what only a great film artist can do: created another world, with possibilities we might otherwise have found inconceivable, and a naturalness we might otherwise have found unimaginable.

A Laughing Matter

Pulp Fiction, 1994

IF YOU TAKE NO PLEASURE IN POPULAR culture, with all its manic excesses, then you are likely to be bewildered, even offended, by Quentin Tarantino's extraordinary film *Pulp Fiction*. Tarantino unapologetically enjoys popular culture at the same time that he satirizes it. Unfortunately, he also seems to specialize in violence.

Violence in film is a serious matter, and for some it is an inexcusable offense. For them, there can be no justification, for example, for the scene in which John Travolta's character accidentally blows a young man's brains out. Even worse, when the movie played in theaters, most of the audience laughed despite the spatter of blood and brain tissue—and with spontane-ous amusement, not the nervous hysteria often provoked by horror films. The violence of *Pulp Fiction* is essential to its aesthetic; though he knew that many would complain, Tarantino meant the audience to laugh.

Yet taken on its own terms, *Pulp Fiction* is a rare accomplishment; it opens a new aesthetic horizon in film. Deliberately violating the con-ventions of action films, Tarantino reimagines stylized moments of violence and exaggerates them until they are almost surrealistic. When most directors would be building tension and suspense, Tarantino has his killers chatting. When most directors would cut away from the violence, Tarantino stays with the aftermath.

What Tarantino has crafted in this film can be best appreciated in the performance he has extracted from John Travolta. One might have concluded that Travolta was too old, too fat, and too far over the hill for *Pulp Fiction*. But he is brilliantly cast; everything wrong about him is right for this part. Seventeen years after *Saturday Night Fever*, his broad mouth and high cheekbones are now bejowled, but there is a promise of sensuality in that ruined face. He still has a teenager's winning vulnerability. His appealing and familiar presence brings just the feel of movie nostalgia Tarantino wanted.

Travolta plays Vincent Vega, a laid-back, get-along kind of guy who is living a depraved and drug-addicted life as a paid killer, but who has an astonishingly innocent soul—as do most of Tarantino's lowlife characters. This innocence in depravity is *Pulp Fiction*'s central theme. It keeps the film from being an exercise in sado-masochistic perversity; it is the source of its humor and its creative energy. It takes the dead genre of film noir and gives it new life.

The film title *Pulp Fiction* harks back to the 1930s and 1940s, when newsstands featured an array of monthly short-story magazines. Among the most popular were those about hard-nosed private investigators. With authors such as Dashiell Hammett, Raymond Chandler, and James M. Cain, these stories were the forerunners of the dark, urban crime movies that became film noir. The stories typically began in the front of the magazine, competing for the reader's attention, and were continued in the back. Though Tarantino would not be old enough to remember this genre, he has constructed his film in a similar way.

We begin with one short story: a hopped-up British couple (played by Amanda Plummer and Tim Roth) decide to rob the coffee shop where they are having breakfast. Before they do, we turn the page—a dark screen—to the next story, about Vincent and Jules (Samuel L. Jackson) going off to retrieve a mysterious briefcase and kill some drug dealers who didn't pay off their boss. Then another dark screen, to the childhood of Butch (Bruce Willis) who grows up to be the boxer who refuses to throw the fight. Unlike the old pulp-fiction magazines, the triptych of stories eventually comes together, interwoven by coincidence and Tarantino's central theme. Set in Los Angeles, it may owe more to Robert Altman's *Short Cuts* or his brilliant *Nashville* than to pulp-fiction magazines.

But Tarantino's borrowings are no defect. He is winking at his audience; he wants them to be aware of his references. Once you figure out the puzzle, it becomes clear that Tarantino is playing with film convention, rather than rejecting or deconstructing it. And his startling humor takes the film beyond anything he has drawn from others.

Yet there can be no doubt that Tarantino intends to shock his audience with graphic violence. European filmmakers are concerned that violence in American film, like pornography, appeals to the lowest common denominator and, like American fast food, is destroying the taste for better things. Some psychologists believe that film and television violence teach America's young people to be violent, or at the very least inure them to real-life violence. Perhaps a more troubling idea is that graphic violence, like pornography, exploits a base instinct that degrades rather than edifies. These reactions to screen violence are too important to be dismissed, but I do not believe that Tarantino has dismissed them. He is neither lacking in moral sensibility nor, even though he wallows in popular culture, a Philistine.

If violence is a form of pornography, then like pornography it presents the problem of drawing lines between exploiting our passions and edifying them. But as modern courts have recognized, it is necessary to go beyond a simple categorical distinction and ask whether an admittedly exploitive work of art has redeeming social value.

This is not to say that Tarantino intends to redeem the violence. He seems to be mocking the arbiters of good taste with his "wicked" humor. This is most blatant in the quirky introduction to Butch's story. Christopher Walken makes a brief appearance in *Pulp Fiction* as a former Vietnam POW. He has come to deliver his dead cellmate's gold watch to the young boy who never knew his father. The Walken character begins to tell the boy what happened to his father in standard heroic rhetoric, but then veers perversely into a description of the intestinal orifice where the father hid the watch, and the intestinal disorders that complicated its concealment.

It is an account that no sane adult would give a child. And while other directors are capable of imagining such a scene, Tarantino was brash enough to keep it in his film. Like toilet graffiti it can be understood as an example of adolescent bad taste, and Tarantino knows that. It is "gross," it is inappropriate, it is irreverent, and one can understand why the younger generation would be warning their fuddy-duddy parents about this film. (Indeed, a surprising number of my middle-aged friends report that their teenage children love it but have warned them that they will hate it.) As Tarantino's script ventures into scatology, he gives the finger to the false nobility of war clichés. But Tarantino is interested less in making an anti-war gesture than sending up a movie cliché. Similarly, this is not an anti-violence film. It is a send-up of movie violence.

ONE ASTUTE TEENAGE CRITIC REMARKED that Tarantino learned something from his first film, *Reservoir Dogs*. All the guys in her high school loved the macho violence but there was not much in this film for her and her female friends. Despite its violence, *Pulp Fiction* has something for women, particularly the scenes between Vincent and Mia.

Mia (Uma Thurman) is the black crime boss's white wife who Vincent is required to entertain. The previous man charged with this task gave her a foot massage; the boss took umbrage and had the massager thrown out of a four-story window. The Vincent-Mia episode quickly turns into an over-the-top parody of a blind date. Vincent prepares himself by going to his drug dealer for a batch of the ultimate hit—a mixture of cocaine and heroin that only a seasoned addict could tolerate. Vincent mainlines the stuff the way a nervous guy might take a drink to boost his confidence before a date. Meanwhile, Mia is sniffing cocaine, not because she's uneasy, but because she is a man-eater whetting her appetite.

Mia takes Vincent to a dance contest, where they do the twist, to the delight of *Saturday Night Fever* fans. Tarantino's elaborate set features vintage 1950s convertibles as booths, pop-icon look-alikes as servers, top-of-the-charts music, all so extravagant in its evocation of nostalgia as to be surreal. The scene is somehow true to the spirit of the film as a whole, parodying popular culture without ever condescending to those who take pleasure in it.

The sexual tension escalates as Mia and Vincent tango back into her home at the end of the evening. But while Vincent is in the toilet (he is always in the toilet at critical moments) Mia finds his drug stash, snorts it, and overdoses. Instead of a sexual conclusion, the evening ends with a slapstick resuscitation involving a huge syringe. In this scene it becomes clear that Vincent and his lowlife friends are essentially overaged adolescents. Indeed, the whole film has the spirit, energy, and sensibility of adolescence. No wonder teenagers love it.

The soundtrack of the very first scene is filled with *motherfuckers*. Amanda Plummer, who was born to play Ophelia, is a crazed Honey Bunny to Tim Roth's Pumpkin. They are two waifs holding hands in the storm, strung out on drugs and sticking up liquor stores for a living. Jules, as Vincent's hit-man partner, sustains this tone. Jackson is a fine match for Travolta; he has a face that looks different from every camera angle, and he radiates strength. Vincent and Jules engage in an earnest discussion about the European nomenclature of American fast food and then a subtle analysis of the sexual significance of the foot massage as they make their way to the apartment where they will kill three men. Jules miraculously eludes a fusillade of bullets. As they leave, they debate whether he was saved by divine intervention or simple luck. Jules, who quotes from Ezekiel to spellbinding effect when he kills people, suddenly understands his Biblical text in a quite different way. As it turns out, his life, and perhaps—if it is possible for a killer—his soul, will be saved by this epiphany.

This theme of redemption is present in each of the three stories. Butch rescues his would-be killer, the black crime boss, from honkey rapists. Butch, who was to be their next victim, has the opportunity to escape, but goes back. Redeemed by this act of solidarity, he is forgiven by the crime boss for not throwing the fight and is sent on his way.

The British couple are also saved. They try to rob Jules, who has ended up in the restaurant where the film began. He has drawn his gun under the table and could easily blow them both away. Instead, in the spirit of justice and honor that prevails among the lowlifes in this film, Jules does the right thing. He stares the amateur criminals down, letting them take his own money but not the mysterious briefcase that he is dutifully returning to the crime boss. We believe that the couple is capable of a killing rampage in the restaurant—Amanda Plummer is a remarkable sight standing on a restaurant table screaming obscenities and waving a Saturday-night special. We also know that the day before, Jules would have killed them without blinking an eye, and that he will have to kill them today if they try to take the briefcase. But Jules sends the couple peacefully out of the restaurant clutching each other and a trash bag filled with stolen money.

But the best scenes of the film involve Jules and Vincent. When they are not killing, they are like college sophomores—both amateur philosophers eager to share their ideas and experiences. The improbable juxtaposition of their earnest dialogue and the homicidal violence is the stylistic twist that allows us to laugh at the explosion of brains and blood in the backseat of their car. Vincent reacts like a teenager unjustly blamed by his buddy for accidentally spilling a beer. And like children of overindulgent parents, they have no idea how to clean up the mess.

Yes, they seem oblivious to the fact that a person has been killed. But their absurd dialogue unexpectedly transforms the meaning of the violence. If Tarantino wanted to defend his film, this could be the foundation of his strongest arguments. *Pulp Fiction* unmasks the macho myth by making it laughable and deheroicizes the kind of violence glorified by Hollywood violence. Tarantino is irreverent, not didactic. He goes from Road Runner cartoon violence to sadistic homosexual rape that silences the laughter. Tarantino will stop at nothing and yet never loses control. He dives into a nightmare and comes up with something funny, taking his audience up and down with him. Though Tarantino thinks his screenplay is funny and would be disappointed if no one laughed, he doesn't consider *Pulp Fiction* a comedy. He is quite right; but if you don't get the humor, you may not like this extraordinary movie.

Seeing Pink

Ma Vie en Rose, 1997

THE BELGIAN-BORN DIRECTOR ALAIN Berliner's *Ma Vie en Rose* has no action, no violence, no romance, no aliens, no natural disasters—not even a recognizable star. It is certainly no comedy and, though it is a film about children, many parents will not want their children to see it. In fact, one wonders who the target audience might have been. Yet in a world that genuinely prized, rather than just tolerated, difference, this film would have been made by Disney. This story of a seven-year-old French boy who is convinced that he is meant to be a girl is, to my knowledge, the first cinematic exploration of gender identity in young children; and it marks a new, truthful departure in cinematic understanding of difference in human sexuality.

Films about sexual identity and difference are now commonplace, and straight audiences seem to take them in stride. Are we now more tolerant, more empathic, more able to respond emotionally to gay and lesbian eroticism? Or have audiences—though more tolerant—become as inured to gay and gender-bending images as they are to violence? Open-mindedness is not quite empathy: empathy demands an identification with the other that permits a vicarious and transformative experience. And film has the capacity to either deepen and purify the emotions or deaden the sensibilities. The outcome depends on both the filmmaker and his audience.

My Beautiful Laundrette (1985), for example, was a modern *Romeo and Juliet* set in South London in which the star-crossed lovers were two men, a Pakistani and a skinhead; the film plumbed the depths of every man's unconscious sexual feelings and demanded a human response. Gay men could go to this film and feel aroused, and straight men, if they allowed themselves, could understand how this was possible.

Ma Vie en Rose is not as challenging as *My Beautiful Laundrette*. Still, it is a major achievement. Ludovic has the innocence of every other seven-year-old child. It is impossible not to empathize with him.

Ludovic is the youngest of four children in a French family that has finally begun to solve its financial problems. We learn that Ludovic's father, Pierre, has become friendly with his boss (and neighbor), who has personally assured him that even in the face of downsizing, Pierre's good job will be secure. The family has just moved into the French equivalent of Levittown and are preparing for a housewarming. After years of skimping, Ludovic's parents are in a celebratory mood as they prepare to greet their new neighbors.

From the start Berliner shows us that every family has its knots and tangles. In the new middle-class neighborhood we see glimpses of the tension and grief that lie behind other familes' ranch-house doors. Pierre's boss and his wife have lost one of their children. The mother has preserved her daughter's room as a shrine to her inconsolable loss. Her husband and son must bear this burden of grief at the center of their shared lives. As we meet the neighbors we also see a long-haired child putting on large dangling earrings and daubing on lipstick in front of a mirror. We think we are watching a little girl playing dress-up. But this is Ludovic, innocently preparing to impress his new neighbors with his girlish beauty. The housewarming is to be his "coming out."

Rather than imposing a directorial will on this material, Berliner finds his way in it from a child's perspective. We see children's programs on French television and segments that look like commercials. We see Ludovic's fantasies:

a mix of television and fairy tale created out of computer graphics.

Berliner wraps his film in pink. Its title suggests Edith Piaf's "La Vie en Rose"—a song about how life is rose-colored when one is in love. But pink is also the color of girlishness, and from the film's first moments, the cinematography indulges various shades of pink, including the pinks of the nursery and the "flesh-colored" pinks of plastic children's dolls. Ludovic's television fairy godmother comes on in a haze of computerized pink, her ample pink bosom barely contained in its pink décolletage. She moves from cartoon figure to real person before our eyes in imaginatively constructed cinematography.

But girl-boys, to use Ludovic's term, are not just imaginative constructions. The "effeminate boy," as he is known in the psychiatric literature, is one of the most persuasive demonstrations that gender identity is biologically given. The girl-boy has the gait, habitus, and gender-distinctive mannerisms of the girl-girl, and it all seems to be innate rather than acquired. Ludovic's own imaginative theory is that when his chromosomes came down the chimney his Ys accidentally got knocked off. Whatever the explanation, girl-boys are a source of humiliation for their parents and objects of torment for their peers; they retreat into a fantasy world for consolation. And as this film poignantly suggests, neither the child nor his parents can be blamed.

Predictably, Ludovic's "coming out" shocks the neighbors, though Pierre adroitly covers it up by declaring that his youngest son is a great joker. But Ludovic's conviction that he is meant to be a girl is no joke. A determined transvestite, he puts his short pants on with the fly in the back. He is fearful and awkward at soccer. Worst of all, he picks the son of Pierre's boss to be his boyfriend, and, violating the shrine of the dead daughter, puts on her communion dress and stages a make-believe wedding. The grieving mother discovers the ceremony and is devastated by the sacrilege. Pierre's boss and the neighbors turn on Ludovic and his family. The bewildered child is derided as a *"tapette"*—French slang for "faggot." One sign of Ludovic's innocence is that he understands only the word's literal meaning, and asks his parents why people are calling him a fly swatter.

Ludovic's parents are ashamed and indignant. They try everything. They consult a child psychologist, who wonders whether they may have wanted a girl. The psychologist's question makes Ludovic's mother feel guilty enough to cut his hair, but her mothering obviously doesn't explain his behavior. Eventually the child psychologist gives up, acknowledging that therapy is useless since her patient has no interest in being cured. By then, Ludovic has been thrown out of grade school. He is the moral leper of the neighborhood and the cause of conflict and resentment in his family since his parents blame each other for his behavior.

Pierre's boss worries that his son is fond of Ludovic and has been corrupted. The bottom falls out when Pierre loses his job.

At the moment of total disaster, Ludovic's family rallies round him: whatever he is, he is their child. Still, they want him back in the closet. Escaping suburbia, they move to Clermont-Ferrand, hoping that Ludovic will be able to suppress his girl-boy nature and allow them to make a fresh start as a normal family. Though it makes him unhappy, Ludovic makes an effort to act like a boy. One day as the friendless child is mooning around by himself, he is set upon by a bully who wants him to play and reacts by retreating into his fantasy world: across the highway is a billboard bearing the likeness of his television fairy godmother; a ladder left behind by workers beckons him to it. In a dreamlike scene we see Ludovic climb up the ladder and escape into a happy pink fantasy. His worried mother goes looking for him. Something tells her to go up the ladder, and the sequence suggests that mother and son will be united by sharing Ludovic's imaginative world. Who can doubt the wisdom of this unity?

Berliner might have ended his story inside the billboard, but he continues until he finds a kind of solution in the real world. The young bully who picked on Ludovic and wanted him to play turns out to be a tomboy. (As Berliner rightly recognizes, tomboys or boy-girls are much less shocking in our patriarchal world than girl-boys.) The bully's mother invites Ludovic and his family to her daughter's dress-up birthday party. Ludovic has to wear a manly costume, and the tomboy, miserable in her princess gown, gets Ludovic into a shed, overcomes his desperate resistance, and changes clothes with him. When the bedraggled Ludovic shows up as a princess, his outraged parents are ready to set upon him. This time, however, the tomgirl's mother intervenes, and the bully confesses that it was all her fault.

Ludovic and his family are saved from social exile. Clermont-Ferrand, it seems, is more tolerant of gender-bending than suburbia. The boy-girl has saved the girl-boy.

But his moment of symmetry is not a happy ending: we do not expect Ludovic's life to be an easy one. And yet perhaps, like Piaf, he will use his imagination to find community in his own creation.

Selling (Out)
Nabokov

Lolita, 1997

VLADIMIR NABOKOV, WHO WAS ABLE TO retire from teaching on the sales of *Lolita*, said he was being "kept by a 12-year-old girl." In a way he was right. *Lolita* sold so many copies because of the double-barreled hype of taboo-breaking sexuality and high art. Not that all those copies were read. *Lolita*, despite its pedophiliac plot, offers no payoff, no pornographic (in Nabokov's words) "copulation of clichés." What is sublime readers will find only with considerable effort. Every paragraph is steeped in arcane literary-cultural-philological allusions. One Nabokov scholar aptly described *Lolita*'s sexual appeal as an "erotic under lock and key, buried deep in the library stacks."

Why, then, make a film of *Lolita*? The visual images of film are an affront to the subtlety and complexity of Nabokovian language. To his credit, Stephen Schiff, who wrote the screenplay, clearly recognized the problem. "I would never claim that we are filming Vladimir Nabokov's *Lolita*. I would say only that we are attempting to translate into a kind of exciting sign language—the language of film—what one of the century's greatest masters of prose rendered so incomparably on the page." Unfortunately, everything greatest about the master has been lost in Schiff's failed and bowdlerized translation.

To be sure, perfect translations from language into images are nearly impossible. But the new Lolita fails even to give what the directors of *Howard's End*, *Sense and Sensibility*, *The Wings of the Dove*, and *Les Miserables* achieved: a feeling for the magic of the original. Nor is the "sign language" medium of film implacably hostile to intellectual depth, as Hal Hartley showed with his brilliant and uncondescending *Henry Fool*. But *Lolita* is relentlessly shallow.

The commercial success of the director Adrian Lyne's previous films (*Flashdance, Fatal Attraction, Indecent Proposal*) allowed him to set his aesthetic sights higher. When he chose Nabokov's *Lolita*, he knew he faced a large challenge, greater still because he would have to distinguish it from Stanley Kubrick's 1962 *Lolita*, for which Nabokov wrote the screenplay.

Kubrick's *Lolita*, now considered something of a milestone in modern filmmaking, was notable for its over-the-top acting, its weird humor (Pauline Kael dubbed it "black slapstick"), and the decision to foreground Peter Sellers as Quilty. Shelley Winters gave a superb performance as Lolita's absurdly hysterical mother; no film makes better use of her shrill talents. James Mason *was* the Humbert Humbert of the novel and an unexpectedly perfect comic foil for Sellers. The improbable contest between the two pedophiles, which lurks in the shadows of the novel, takes the spotlight in Kubrick's film. It was not the novel, but one could hear Vladimir Nabokov's unmistakable voice in the new medium. And Kubrick had the sly wit to put a conspicuous but unidentified picture of Nabokov on the wall in the scene of the fatal confrontation between Quilty and Humbert. This is exactly the kind of allusion that Nabokov worked into every page of his novel.

When it was released, many critics thought that Kubrick's surreal take on *Lolita* was morally reprehensible. Even the most discerning film critics were offended. Stanley Kauffmann blamed Nabokov for a screenplay that was condescending to the film medium. Pauline Kael reports that Reinhold Niebuhr, the leading American theologian of the day, obviously did not understand Kubrick's film or the novel, both of which end with a pregnant Lolita, married to a young man who is literally deaf and oblivious to her sordid past. While careful readers of the novel will know that Lolita the housewife is destined to die in childbirth, Niebuhr wrote uncomprehendingly about this ending as an obscured moral lesson of "Lolita's essential redemption in a happy marriage." And Arthur Schlesinger Jr. weighed in for the American intelligentsia, declaring that Kubrick's film is "not only inhuman, it is antihuman." Kael was one of the few critics who got the joke. In a throwaway line of her review she gave what may be the most illuminating description of Nabokov's novel: "A satire on the myths of love."

Moralists who attack Nabokov for flouting basic moral values and psychologists who want to analyze his characters might do better if they realized that *Lolita* was written to make such attempts seem foolish. Nabokov says he wrote in much the way he composed chess puzzles to support himself as a Russian émigré in Europe—delighting in planting misleading clues. Perhaps even more telling of Nabokov's project is his description in his novel *Ada* of an English music-hall performance. An apparition comes careening onto the stage, defying the laws of gravity and the limits of the human spine. It flips backwards onto its hands and races around until at last a foot reaches down, opening its baggy pants to reveal an acrobat who has brachiambulated (Nabokov's neologism) onto the stage. The audience bursts into applause. This is the essential Nabokov, and the characters in *Lolita* are similar apparitions, meant to defy the laws of the moral universe and test the limits of human psychology, all for the sake of artistry. Nabokov was not interested in creating believable and psychologically real characters or developing real relationships between them.

Nabokov thinks the unthinkable and then describes it in detail. For those who doubt this and want to read *Lolita* as a love story, consider the novel's study-hall scene. Humbert Humbert, sexually obsessed and insatiable, pays Lolita 65 cents to masturbate him while he ogles the white neck of her schoolmate who is engrossed in a book. He confides to the reader he cannot resist because he may never again have such an opportunity. The scene is typical of the novel and seems to have been borrowed from Havelock Ellis. Nabokov had a high regard for Ellis, who collected and recorded bizarre particulars of exotic perversions in much the same way that Nabokov collected butterflies. *Lolita* mocks middle-class convention but even more the Freudian generalizations about the pedophile and his victim. Nabokov famously despised psychoanalytic generalizations (Freud was "a hot-air balloonist") and the entire "Viennese Delegation." He carried on a war of witticisms with psychoanalysis in all of his writings.

Kubrick's *Lolita* was true to this spirit. Lyne's new *Lolita* gets almost everything wrong. After commissioning and then rejecting screenplays by Harold Pinter and David Mamet, he hired Stephen Schiff, who would help him turn Humbert Humbert into a tormented victim. Theirs is a humorless tale of doomed passion and unreciprocated love with a moral apotheosis: in the end Humbert realizes that he has stolen Lolita's childhood.

It would be absurd to argue that the novel contains nothing of this kind: many of the film's lines are taken verbatim from the text. But Nabokov's trick—and it is a trick—is to put every possibility of a human relationship into Humbert Humbert's self-serving confession. Readers come to have a certain sympathy with Humbert even as they loathe him: Nabokov induced both reactions. By omitting the loathsome half of our ambivalence and the bizarre comedy of the novel, this film defeats Nabokov's genius and sentimentalizes his acerbic wit.

Although the novel contains endless layers of irony, beginning with Humbert Humbert's name, Schiff ignores them all for the sake of psychological realism. Schiff, a longtime film reviewer, knew that you cannot get your foot in the door with mainstream American moviegoers unless you give them someone to identify with. Humbert Humbert is an unlikely candidate for identification—former mental patient, pedophile, alcoholic, snob—but the audience is meant to sympathize with him. We see him enslaved by love and then by the willful Lolita—the victimizer made victim. Jeremy Irons plays his tormented part faultlessly. With Lyne's misguided encouragement, he does everything he can to make Humbert Humbert a psychologically transparent and sympathetic figure. Schiff presents the myth of the pedophile's love as the real thing.

Nabokov would have cringed. His Humbert shares his disdain for the standard psychoanalytic cant about infantile sexuality, pedophilia, and sexual fixation, and naturally, Humbert thrives on playing games with his psychiatrists. He feeds the doctors of a European asylum false dreams and is delighted when they decide he is a homosexual. The novel also mocks the reader who believes such ideas.

Humbert's charming explanation of his own pedophilia is psychologically ridiculous and not meant to be taken seriously. But Lyne and Schiff take the bait, accepting Humbert's account that ties his fixation to his first summer girlfriend. They begin their tragic love story with gauzy scenes of the 12-year-olds, Humbert and Annabel, playing on the Riviera beach. In a voice-over Irons tells us of her shocking death from typhus six months later, and thus we are given a psychological understanding of the traumatized man who can only break Annabel's spell "by incarnating her in another."

The misguided psychological realism influenced Lyne's casting of Dominique Swain as Lolita, Melanie Griffith as her angry mother, and Frank Langella as a degenerate Quilty. Schiff has suggested rather snidely that in Kubrick's *Lolita*, Sue Lyon, at 15 looked like a 20-year-old porn star. He thinks Dominique Swain, also 15 when *Lolita* was filmed, has the virtue of looking like a real girl. Yet she is certainly not diminutive or innocent. She looks like one of those teenagers who have gone from childhood to womanhood by age 12, and share their mothers' sexual sophistication. On the screen she is almost as large as Irons.

She is, however, a minor, and there are scenes simulating sexual intercourse in this film that Kubrick avoided. Even though none of it is crudely pornographic, there should be serious concerns about the psychological effects on a teenage girl of acting out a sexual affair with a man who is supposed to be her stepfather. And what we see is not all of it: Lyne reports that he had a lawyer with him in the cutting room. We know that Kubrick's choice, Sue Lyon, had a troubled life after *Lolita*, and Lyne's press releases report that he sent Swain to a fancy Swiss psychiatrist as a preventive measure. That guarantees nothing, and we may ask whether Dominique Swain's childhood—like that of the film's Lolita—has been stolen.

That question can fairly be asked of the new *Lolita* both because of the realism of the film, and because Schiff's screenplay (unlike Nabokov's novel or Kubrick's film) makes the emotional relationship between the stepfather and the daughter the heart of the story. Nabokov's novel is located in Humbert's self-serving confession, not in the real world. Lolita exists as the pedophile's fantasy, and although his nymphet is often described in obsessive detail (the down in her armpits as she lifts her tennis racket), the picture of an actual child comes through only in those rare moments when Humbert feels a twinge of guilt. Kubrick cools the heat of the visual medium by downplaying Lolita's role, centering on the struggle between the pedophiles. Schiff, in contrast, gives moviegoers believable relationships in which they can get psychologically involved. They see Lolita slowly getting the better of her stepfather, demanding more money in exchange for her sexual favors, then driving him wild with jealousy and leading him across America so she can rendezvous with his rival, Quilty. Not only does she control and exploit Humbert but in the one great (and tragic) irony of the film, she turns out to be actually in love with Quilty—a degenerate who wants her to act in his pornographic films. Again, there is nothing in the scenario that is not in Nabokov's novel, but it is out of context, transforming satire into tragedy.

In truth, the film is very much in the spirit of a short-story version of *Lolita* published by Nabokov's son long after his father's death and presumably without his father's blessing. In it Humbert Humbert seduces his stepdaughter and then commits suicide by walking onto a busy highway at night. This wretched story lacks all of the wit, style, and mind-bending imagination of the novel. Much the same can be said of the new *Lolita*. If Lyne and Schiff manage to enhance their reputations on the basis of this film, they will have done it by selling out Nabokov's.

Happily Ever After
The King of Masks, 1996

A RECENT RUN OF SUCCESSFUL FOREIGN-made films features an affirming "love affair" between parent and child. Two Oscar winners, *Burnt by the Sun* and *Life is Beautiful*, celebrate fathers who are martyrs. Others, such as *Kolya*, *Central Station*, and now *The King of Masks*, portray the falling in love of an adult and a young unrelated and unwanted child. This adult-child "romance" is hardly a new cinematic theme, and it smacks of sentimentality. Pauline Kael complained about it years ago as a trick in foreign films, but it is also a Hollywood staple. And I came out of the theater drying my eyes after seeing *The King of Masks* for the second time. This is a film I could see once a month. It is better than therapy. Yes, *The King of Masks* is sentimental, but in just the way that Dickens is: this is a film to restore one's faith in human nature—your own and other people's. What is better than that?

The director and producer of *The King of Masks*, Wu Tian Ming, is widely regarded as the father of the fifth generation of Chinese filmmakers. (Better known to American audiences is his protégé Zhang Yimou, the director of *Raise the Red Lantern*, *Red Sorghum*, and *The Story of Qiu Ju*.) For years, despite the constraints of censorship, Wu created enough political and economic space for his group, Xi-an Film Studios, to make internationally acclaimed films. Xi-an films are typically fables, period-piece art films safely located in the pre-communist era that preserved the exotic images of old China. Even Wu's *The Old Well* and Zhang's *Story of Qiu Ju*, both set in contemporary China, were timeless narratives about the human predicament. Although some Western critics could find political protest in these fables, the Xi-an filmmakers seemed to have been inspired by the high culture of China's past. And perhaps because they were constrained by censorship, Wu and his fifth generation poured much of their creative energy into their cinematography, which has both the subtlety and the unexpected exuberance of Chinese art.

Wu led this community of accomplished film artists until the 1989 Tiananmen Square demonstrations. As fate would have it, he was in the United States at the time on a lecture tour sponsored by the Chinese-American community. Wu resolved not to return to his homeland. But like other creative émigrés, he languished. After six years of self-imposed exile, including a stint operating a video store, where he subjected himself to a huge dose of American films—he claims 900—Wu went back to his homeland to work again. Though he was unsure about how he would be received, he suffered no political recriminations. The bottom line had become more important than ideology in the new China, and the Xi-an studio had been organized to run like a bureaucratic collective. Wu was free to bring in more talented people, make deals in Hong Kong, and be less concerned about politics and censorship. In this climate Wu's protégé, Zhang, broke loose with a new-edge urban film, *Keep Cool*. When the international community gave it a unanimous thumbs-down, Zhang accused Western critics of trying to pigeonhole Chinese filmmakers. But it may be that the artistic achievement of the Xi-an studio is an example of creativity emerging against the tensions of restraints.

Whatever the temptations of the new freedom, Wu Tian Ming seems immune to them. *The King of Masks* is an allegory about traditional Chinese values, the place of the artist in society, and the possibilities of human connection. It is at the same time a self-portrait—the artist as survivor. *The King of Masks* is set in

Sichuan Province in 1930, a time of conflict between regional warlords and Chiang Kai-shek's Nationalist troops. It was also a time of natural disaster, as rivers flooded and the poor were left starving and homeless.

The screenplay as filmed has a familiar, almost operatic structure. All the characters are introduced in the first few scenes in a cinematic overture. There is love at first sight, tragic misunderstanding, character transformation, and a play within the screenplay that is crucial to the plot and coda of a happy ending. There may be nothing new in the parent-child romance, but *The King of Masks* evokes an astonishing emotional intensity of the theme's greatest portrayals.

According to Hegel, the original portrayals in Western culture—and indeed of all romantic art—were the paintings of the Madonna and Child, where the beholder was invited to enter into the sacred spirit of love depicted in Mary's gaze. In life as in art, romantic love means entering into and sharing an emotional union—love as a transcending of the self. Romantic love between adults is more difficult to achieve because it entails reciprocity in the transcendence of self. In the 20th century, such romantic love is the utopian antidote for our existential loneliness. Everyone is looking for it, and, indeed, lasting reciprocal love between adults today is a miracle. Many have lost faith and have returned in life and in art to the parent-child variation.

In Wu's version, the King of Masks, an old street performer, has learned through years of practice to change masks with the speed and skill of a magician. To the people who gather around him it is a trick. But the King of Masks is a consummate artist and the last practitioner of a traditional art form that will die with him if he finds no disciple. His tradition also requires that the secrets of his art be passed on to a son. But his only son died in childhood, and his wife has long since abandoned him.

The King of Masks moves through Sichuan Province in a houseboat on the river. His trained monkey is his only companion. Wu seems to have exploited every mannerism of his animal actor to a good purpose. I emphasize this in the hope of suggesting the uncanny genius of Wu's direction. There is the frantic pacing back and forth, used by Wu to convey the mood of desperation; the quizzical, almost human expression that asks what these people are doing; the shrieks and jumping up and down when the child accidentally sets the houseboat on fire. Every emotional passage in the film is marked by this trained monkey as if it were a kind of Greek chorus.

Wu cast Zhu (of the Beijing People's Artistic Theater) as the King of Masks and the eight-year-old Zhou Renying as Doggie because they were in real life what they were to be in his film. Zhu is tall, lean, and aged but not bent, with a missing front tooth that somehow adds to his dignity. He has been performing for over 40 years and has endured every adversity, including the Cultural Revolution. Zhou Renying was a member of the Xi-an Acrobatic Troupe. Sent there by her very poor family when she was three years old, she grew up without parental nurturing. The third central actor in the film, Zhao Zhigang, is in real life "the Prince of the Shaoxing Opera." Wu cast him as Master Liang, the celebrated female impersonator of the Sichuan Opera. Zhao conveys a sense of resignation and regret as though his masculinity has been imprisoned in an unwanted, if celebrated, female identity. All three are in some sense social outcasts, the lonely street performer, the unwanted girl, and the rich and famous Master Liang trapped in his female impersonation.

The King of Masks is a proud artist, who knows his own value even if no one else does. But behind the old man's pride we see the shadows of his loneliness. In a Sichuan Province shaken by war and ravaged by floods starving parents are selling their sons and giving their daughters away to anyone who promises the child a home. The King of Masks does not want the daughters who are thrust at him by their mothers; he wants a son. Then a child's voice cries out "Yeh Yeh"—"grandfather" in Chinese. "Yeh Yeh" will echo in your mind after seeing this film, as Doggie utters it with every different emotion of which a child is capable. This first "Yeh Yeh" causes the King of Masks to turn back and behold just the little boy he wants. Here is the miracle of love at first sight. A price is agreed upon, and, after buying Doggie new clothes, he triumphantly takes the child to his little houseboat on the riverbank.

The monkey greets the child with a show of displeasure—sibling rivalry?—but soon man and monkey have succumbed to the new arrival. The child warms to the King's kindness, and both allow themselves to be vulnerable. This is the crucial moment in every love affair, when the defensive armor is let down. This does not come easy to either of these would-be lovers, even though it looks like a match made in heaven. Doggie, as we will soon discover, is a girl pretending to be a boy so that the dealer could sell her for a price. She had already been in several homes where she had been abused, so she has reasons to be defensive and distrusting. Like many would-be lovers, she has a secret that she is not prepared to tell. And the King, in taking Doggie into his life, is giving up years of self-sufficiency. Now, as Doggie scratches his back where he cannot reach, he throws his backscratcher into the river to seal his commitment to their love affair. When he discovers the deception he will be outraged.

The King of Masks is about traditions—their ability to give structure and meaning, and their tendency to oppress. The King of Masks and Master Liang may be outcasts, but they practice traditional art forms that bring a little warmth to cold reality. Their belief in their artistic traditions is what unites and protects them from the self-interested cynicism that surrounds them. (One can not help but believe that this is the director's account and justification for what he has done with his own life.) But tradition also has the King of Masks believe that he cannot bequeath his art to Doggie. She has his talent and wants to be his apprentice. We can see that these two were made for each other, and only his and China's patriarchal tradition interferes with their union.

Part of Doggie's irresistible charm is that she is both naive about the power of the tradition and indignant as to why a "teapot spout" should make such a difference. Wu sets this innocent conviction against China's patriarchal tradition, and its history of female infanticide, that echoes into this century. Will this indignant little girl conquer an age-old tradition for everyone's benefit?

The resolution of Doggie's gender imposture will require the intervention of Master Liang, who lives between the categories and mediates between male and female. Master Liang befriends the King of Masks and invites him and Doggie to a Chinese Opera about filial love in which he plays a daughter who leaps into the pits of hell to save her father and is reborn as the living Bodhisattva. In the Buddhist tradition of China, the Bodhisattva is worshiped as a deity because on the verge of Nirvana the Bodhisattva renounced bliss out of compassion for others.

The Chinese language has a special word for love of a parent: *xiao*. It conveys honor, respect, and obedient love. Doggie, who has never had a parent's love, has become stubborn, determined, and defiant, causing all sorts of calamities to befall the King of Masks as she tries to make him accept her. But after learning *xiao* from Master Liang's performance, she risks her life to save Yeh Yeh from death. She does not die or turn into the living Bodhisattva, but she does make the proud old man unbend and love her. As the film ends we see her practicing with the

King of Masks. We know that his art will not die and that there will be a happily ever after. We also know that both Yeh Yeh and Doggie have broken out of the cage of their characters in order to achieve lasting love.

Confucius said that human nature is the same everywhere; only the customs are different. This is a film that will make you hope he was right.

Redemption

American Beauty, 1999

MOST CRITICS AND FILMGOERS APPEAR TO see *American Beauty* as a black-comic, ironic caricature of dysfunctional suburbia culminating in a weirdo looking at a dead guy and apparently enjoying it. It is easy to see how the movie could produce such reactions. The only "decent" people in it are a couple of gay men, a tax attorney, and an anesthesiologist; only they seem at home in their suburban identities. Virtually everyone else lacks a sense of authenticity and pretends to some quality—self-control, self-confidence, worldliness—that he or she lacks. *American Beauty* unmasks all these pathological deceptions and exposes the hypocrisy of middle-class morality.

But there is more to *American Beauty*—the first film for both its director, Sam Mendes, and its screenwriter, the playwright Alan Ball—than meets the eye. Indeed, the movie is an extended meditation on beauty—its meaning and deep importance. In exploring this theme, the film in effect enacts the views about beauty and ethics advanced by the Harvard literature professor Elaine Scarry in her book *On Beauty and Being Just*. I do not mean to suggest that the filmmakers drew directly on Scarry's ideas. But the resonances are so uncanny that they suggest something more than mere coincidence. Perhaps, in parallel, Scarry and *American Beauty* have touched a chord of mass consciousness—a millennial search for spiritual meaning in beauty.

Scarry has two sets of ideas. One is about the felt experience of beauty: the "surfeit of aliveness," the "decentering" of the self in consciousness, and the flicker from the mind to the body that validates the sentient moment. This is beauty as a wake-up call to the plenitude of life. *American Beauty* presents a similar message. We hear it from Ricky Fitts (Wes Bentley), a teenager who compulsively videotapes everything he sees. And we hear it at the end of the film in a voice-over by Lester Burnham (Kevin Spacey), who has died for it—thankfully, not before he enjoyed a few moments of moral enlightenment.

Scarry's other set of ideas is about the connection between beauty and moral insight. Beauty, she says, "ignites the desire for truth," and is deeply connected to symmetry, fairness, and justice itself. *American Beauty* makes similar connections and goes further, suggesting that spiritual redemption begins with the experience of beauty. Look at beauty and something looks back: perhaps God Himself.

AMERICAN BEAUTY'S PARADIGM OF BEAUTY is neither the young girl who is the eponymous American beauty nor anything else that is conventionally beautiful. It is, improbably enough, a plastic bag. Ricky has videotaped some trash and dead leaves caught in the wind; their dance, a miracle of nature, choreographs inanimate litter into beauty. Ricky tells us that it is the most beautiful thing he has ever seen. The *New York Times* critic Stephen Holden identifies this image as being borrowed from *Variations*, an avant-garde silent film by Nathaniel Dorsky about unconventional and unexpected glimpses of beauty.

Ricky Fitts is the prophet of this religion of beauty. He has survived two years in a mental hospital, where he was incarcerated by his father, an ex-Marine colonel. Colonel Fitts (Chris Cooper) makes George Patton seem like a teddy bear. All his militaristic manliness is fueled by a repressed homosexuality that explodes and destroys. He is the most pathological example of a conventional American man. His wife has been driven into catatonia, and Ricky has escaped into the bliss of beauty.

Like many of his predecessors in film and literature, Ricky, the strange outsider, exposes the madness of normal life. Drugged into zombie-hood by psychiatrists, he now "parties" on the best marijuana and sells it to support his vocation—capturing the world and its unexpected beauty in his video camera. This beauty transcends the quotidian world, aesthetic conventions, the ugliness of the commonplace, and even the horror of death—and he captures it because he has what the philosopher Stuart Hampshire, in a review of Scarry's book, called "the arts of attention."

Beauty has driven fear out of Ricky's world. He will look into the eye of the murdered Lester Burnham with a strange smile of pleasure signaling the "surfeit of aliveness" in the face of death, the validating flicker from the mind to the body as he saw God looking back. The film's script carefully prepares us for this epiphanic moment. Ricky has told Lester's daughter Jane (Thora Birch), with whom he is in love, that beauty grounds the world and his own being. Sometimes, he tells her, when he is aware of all the beauty in the world, he is overwhelmed and feels as though his heart will cave in. Jane loves him, but his only real convert is Lester.

Lester's conversion is the black comedy in the foreground of *American Beauty*. The film begins as it will end, with a voice-over by Lester's spirit: "My name is Lester Burnham. This is my neighborhood. This is my street. This is my life. In less than a year I'll be dead. Of course I don't know that yet. In a way I'm dead already." Lester is a man whose moral adventure seems to have been a failure. Neither in love nor in work can he find meaning. His wife Carolyn (Annette Bening) is a real-estate agent desperately trying to climb the ladder of commercial success. Feeling inadequate and vulnerable, she has become a control freak whose compulsions rule her family and make intimacy impossible. Jane, their only child, despises them both.

If ever a man needed a strong dose of aliveness, Lester Burnham does. Dragged by his wife to a high-school basketball game to show support for Jane, who is one of the cheerleaders, he finds his beauty in another cheerleader, Angela (Mena Suvari), a traditional American beauty and the best friend of his less than conventionally beautiful daughter. But what happens is exactly as if Scarry had staged the scene. Scarry writes, "At the moment one comes into the presence of something beautiful, it greets you. It lifts away from the neutral background as though coming forward to welcome you—as though the object were designed to 'fit' your perception." Just so, we enter Lester's mind and watch as all the other cheerleaders disappear and a spotlight falls on Angela. And his "angel" seems to welcome him as rose petals pour out of her bosom toward him. This moment is, of course, not innocent. The middle-aged father smitten by his daughter's high-school friend is the nightmare of suburbia, and the movie builds tension around the possibility of its consummation.

The American beauty, it turns out, is as dysfunctional as everyone else. Angela thinks that sophistication consists in the easy use of foul language and talk about sexual experiences. She presents herself as an aspiring model and feigns a worldly willingness to sleep her way to the top. But her coarseness and cynicism conceal an immaturity and utter lack of self-confidence. She is terrified of being plain and ordinary. Her friend Jane accepts all of Angela's pretenses until Ricky comes into the picture and, with his discerning eye and his nonstop video taping, reveals the truth. Jane becomes the swan, Angela the ugly duckling.

Still, beauty ignites Lester's desire for something better. He quits his job, thumbs his nose at his wife's compulsions, and retreats to his last remembered time of happiness, even aliveness—adolescence, in the 1960s. Ricky helps him along by introducing him to the best weed on the planet. He gets high, works out, buys a red Pontiac, finds a job in a fast-food drive-through, and generally chills. All this animation outrages his wife, who starts an affair charged with excitement but devoid of love or beauty.

Her father's behavior and her mother's cynical advice—in life you can only count on yourself—drives Jane into the arms of Ricky Fitts. When Jane wishes her father dead, Ricky offers to kill him. Is he bluffing? Meanwhile, Lester's wife has learned the ecstasy of firing a gun from her partner in adultery and has mastered a motivational tape mantra: "I will not be a victim." She, too, is thinking of killing Lester. And Colonel Fitts, after seeing what he takes to be a homosexual encounter between Ricky and Lester (it is really a drug transaction), batters his son in a homophobic rage—and then succumbs to his own homosexual urges. The extraordinary moment when he embraces and kisses Lester on the lips is difficult to forget. When Lester, now as chilled out as a man can get, gently refuses his sexual advances, the colonel suffers the kind of humiliation that engenders homicidal thoughts.

While everyone is thinking about killing him, Lester finally gets his chance with the American beauty. When the seduction begins, the girl of his dreams reveals that she is a virgin. If discovering her was a wake-up call, this is his moment of grace and moral enlightenment. He has an even more powerful decentering experience as he becomes aware of his own instinctive goodness. He refuses to take the young girl's virginity, and this act opens another world to him. Suddenly he is alive to the beauty of life, to truth, to justice, and to his love of his own family. Beauty has not distracted him from the world but made him more attentive to it. He reassures Angela that she is far from ordinary—that she is, in fact, beautiful—and allows her a moment of human intimacy when she sets aside her pretenses. He is now able to think about his daughter Jane as a real person and is delighted to learn she is in love with Ricky. He picks up a picture of his family, and we see him enthusing about beauty and having that ecstatic flicker from the mind to the body.

In that instant, he is shot. As Ricky peers into the dead man's eye, Lester's conversion to the aesthetic of redemptive beauty is revealed to us. The moment before you die, Lester tells us in his spirit's final voice-over, is not an instant in which your whole life passes before you—the moment goes on and on. Out of this infinitude Lester speaks about the beauty of life, and with "the arts of attention" now at his command, he describes how every moment of his life was filled with beauty. Like Ricky, he now speaks of seeing the beauty behind everything. He reprises Ricky's version of the world's overflowing beauty in a more hopeful way: there is so much beauty in the world that he feels his heart will burst and then instead there is rain everywhere.

Leo Tolstoy wrote that unlike happy families, who are all the same, unhappy families are unhappy in different ways. What eludes filmmakers today, as it did Tolstoy, are the particulars for a believably happy family. *American Beauty* does not have a formula, but it offers the possibility of something better, if only for one redemptive moment that might go on forever in a possible hereafter.

The remaining mystery, however, and for my interpretation of it, is that most of the audience does not see beauty in the miracle of the trash dance. Garbage is garbage, Angela is a wanna-be sophisticate, and Ricky is a wacked-out drug dealer. Most viewers cannot adjust their aesthetic perceptions. Art and beauty have always been about finding the universal in the particular, but sometimes it is not easily found. Scarry and Ricky Fitts find beauty because they are artists in the arts of attention; in that sense beauty is in the praxis of the beholder. It takes an effort of the will, the heart, and the mind to experience the wake-up call. Beauty can ignite all sorts of desires, but *American Beauty* suggests that some other alchemy of human nature, something more than beauty itself, is needed to draw virtue from the flames.

Feet of Clay

Thirteen Days, 2000

No more than ten people were in the audience at the afternoon showing of *Thirteen Days*. My brother and I had gone to the film to relax. We had both lived through the 1962 Cuban Missile Crisis, when America had been on the brink of nuclear war with the Soviet Union, and you wondered whether you were a fool not to have built a bomb shelter for your family. But the events had been replayed many times before. The Cuban Missile Crisis now ranks among the most carefully documented events of the Cold War. So how could *Thirteen Days* be made suspenseful? But it was. My brother and I emerged from the movie dewy-eyed with tears of relief as we once again realized how close the world had come to Armageddon.

Despite my emotional reaction, my critical faculties told me I was watching a "Classic Comics" docudrama in which the cast was not acting but impersonating real people—and not doing a good job. Bruce Greenwood played Jack Kennedy but could not summon up the president's aura; Steven Culp played Bobby Kennedy with a disconcerting effeminacy; and Kevin Costner, who starred as presidential assistant Kenny O'Donnell, had a ridiculous version of a Boston accent and, in a Hollywood rewriting of history, became a central player in the crisis. Still, my reason failed to protect my psyche.

In part, my reaction owed to the psychological craft of the director, Roger Donaldson. But it was also a consequence of having lived through the days when the possibility of nuclear holocaust seemed real (in fact, as the financial backers had feared, the younger audience stayed away). Such experiences are never completely forgotten; they settle into the unconscious. Atomic explosions became an archetypal vision of the apocalypse, and they are the dramatic crux of the film. The opening image is a special-effects mushroom cloud, somehow more horrifying because of its beauty. This is followed by the rapid firing of a swarm of surface-to-air missiles, an ICBM launch, and a mysterious projectile hurtling through space. Before the mind can assimilate these images, the brain jumps to the possibility of a world-ending nuclear war. Then that mysterious projectile swoops away and resolves into the fuselage of a U2 spy plane. We watch it fly over Cuba, photograph the Soviet missiles, and set the crisis in motion.

And lest your attention wander, the director uses this psychological device at repeated intervals. Halfway through the film, he suddenly interposes another atomic explosion. This time a massive hydrogen bomb lifts its man-made plumes until they tower over the natural clouds.

Has Donaldson gone overboard? Are we to be shown how the war of nerves could have ended? No, this is not fiction. David Self's screenplay narrative has based each of these terrifying visual moments on actual events: the Atomic Energy Commission went forward with a scheduled hydrogen-bomb test in the Pacific during the crisis without considering the possibility that it might seem a provocation to nervous Kremlin generals.

THERE WERE OTHER PROVOCATIONS THAT JFK never intended—indeed, more than the director includes. Some were accidental, but the premise of *Thirteen Days* is that Maxwell Taylor and other hawks in the Pentagon were eager to provoke the Russians into World War III—and would have, had it not been for Jack and Bobby Kennedy and their only loyal friend in the White House, Kenny O'Donnell. In *Thirteen Days*, these three Irish Catholics from Massachusetts save the world from nuclear holocaust.

And they have to fight the WASP Washington establishment, their own cabinet, the CIA, and Congress—as well as Khrushchev—to do it.

(The film unfortunately says nothing about the events leading up to the crisis. In *Thirteen Days* Soviet hard-liners move offensive missiles to Cuba without any American provocation. No one doubts that the crisis is real and that something must be done about it: a surgical strike by the Air Force on the missile sites, a full-scale invasion of Cuba, or both. Yet in *The Kennedy Tapes*, a book of transcripts of secretly taped White House deliberations, the president asks his experts whether 40 missiles really make that much difference, given all the other Soviet ICBMs that were already aimed at America. He does not get a direct answer, but Soviet missiles in Cuba meant that a Russian first strike could destroy the majority of Americans in five minutes rather than half an hour. Of course, America had missiles in Turkey that could do the same to them. Both sides ultimately backed off, though our concession on the Turkish missiles was not made public at the time. JFK had not been as tough as the public thought.)

The worst warmonger in the film is stogie-chewing Air Force General Curtis LeMay (Kevin Conway). Like Dean Acheson (who was brought in because he knows the Soviets), LeMay thinks the Kennedy boys take after their father, who as U.S. ambassador to England favored American isolationism and appeasement of Hitler. When the Kennedys hesitate about preemptive strikes on the missile sites, these warmongers think it is simply more of the same. Their naive caution is set against the supposed experts—Acheson, John McCone of the CIA, and the Joint Chiefs of Staff—who are ready to bring on World War III. In the film, JFK has to bypass the military chain of command to keep the chiefs of staff from starting a war. The president takes it upon himself to give direct orders to American military men on the scene. Kenny O'Donnell shares part of that responsibility in the film: he calls Commander Ecker before his low-altitude flight over Cuba and warns him that he is not to be shot at because General LeMay will retaliate and start a war. Ecker is, indeed, shot at, and upon landing attributes the bullet holes in his plane to a flock of sparrows.

The O'Donnell telephone conversations may be the best part of the film: they bring the crisis into the compass of ordinary human experience. Costner, as the president's assistant, calls from the White House just as the pilots are about to go off on their missions. They know they are risking their lives to do their job, and Costner gives them something to die for—the prevention of World War III.

We have no reason to believe that Kenny O'Donnell actually did any of the things he is portrayed doing in this film. McNamara and Sorenson both report that he was never in the room during their deliberations. And I doubt, for example, that he had the kind of personal relationship with JFK that is depicted in the film. But Costner's role is to be the everyman. He puts his faith in his best friend Bobby, who makes the crucial deal with Anatoly Dobrynin, the Soviet ambassador, that convinces Khrushchev to remove the Soviet missiles.

THERE'S MORE THOUGH, TO MY EMOTIONAL response to the film. In my office I have a photograph of the 1947 Harvard varsity football team. The good friends of the film as they were in real life—Bobby Kennedy, the attorney general, and Kenny O'Donnell, the president's assistant—are seated on either end of the second row; I am in the back. Football players make connections that last a lifetime.

Thirteen Days set off a confrontation between the film's fictive characters and my remembered real ones. Or was it the other way around? Had my memories become fictions, while the Bobby and Kenny up on the screen were the realities? I had never reconciled in my own mind the two young men of the past who had been my Harvard teammates and the men of historical consequence portrayed on the screen. When you know people's feet of clay before they become idols it is difficult to reimagine them. *Thirteen Days* put me to that test.

Anyone who knew Bobby Kennedy knew he was too small to play football. Nonetheless, his football career at Harvard has been made into a legend. According to a recent book, as a senior in 1947 he scored a touchdown against Yale with a broken leg. His teammates will tell you that he did start the first game of that season, even though there were at least eight bigger and better players at his position. He then disappeared from the starting lineup with a mysterious injury, although he kept coming to practice. It seemed his Harvard football career was over when he broke his leg in one of the last scrimmages of the year. But the coach put him in for one play against Yale so he could get his varsity letter. He hobbled down the sidelines on a kickoff with his leg in a cast as everyone on the team held his breath at what seemed to be an insane decision by the coach, and a measure of the Kennedy family's influence. (Teddy, as it turns out, was the only real football player in the family.) Certainly Bobby Kennedy was a fighter, almost foolhardy; he was told to avoid contact on that one play, but insisted on diving in.

Although he lacked the size and ability to be a varsity football player even at Harvard College, Bobby Kennedy was still a presence on that team. He was the first rich and famous person most of us had met. He wore a Chesterfield overcoat and talked with that Kennedy accent, which revealed more about the years at Brahmin private schools and the Court of St. James than it did about the family's Boston Irish heritage. But he was no snob. Even then he was drawn to the have-nots; psychologically he must have felt like one of them. He seemed to care particularly about the returning veterans of World War II, most of them second- and third-generation ethnics who would never have been at Harvard were it not for the GI Bill. Through his father, he got several of them summer jobs and he lent (gave) them money. Still, he was not exactly at ease with them or with any other group. He was painfully shy, and despite the trappings of social sophistication, he was a childlike outsider who seemed never to have belonged to a real peer group. In retrospect, Bobby probably labored under a Kennedy-sized inferiority complex. The runt of the Kennedy litter, he was too small to be a football player and far from a good student. He was probably dyslexic, and he struggled with his studies at Milton Academy and then Harvard and then the University of Virginia Law School. Bobby had no pretensions about his IQ, particularly in comparison to his brother Jack. He would surely have laughed out loud, as I did, when

Stephen Culp, the actor impersonating him in *Thirteen Days*, utters the line, "I hate being called the brilliant one."

Like his mother Rose, whom he resembled, Bobby was serious about his Catholicism. One of my unforgettable memories of those days was a religious debate between the captain of the football team and Bobby. We football players ate together at the Varsity Club after practice, and when Bobby joined us, though he was shy, he was forever getting into arguments. On this occasion he was arguing with the captain, Vincent Moravec, about whether he could go to heaven. Moravec, one of the most decent human beings I have ever met—an opinion I am confident Bobby shared—was a Catholic, and according to Bobby he had irrevocably sinned by marrying a Protestant. Moravec was a huge man with the innocent eyes of a deer, and he was almost weeping as he defended himself against Bobby's inquisitorial arguments. When Moravec refused to concede that he was doomed to rot in hell, an irate Bobby called Archbishop Cushing to settle the matter. Bobby not only knew the phone number by heart, but the archbishop took his call, even though it was almost 11:00 PM. The prelate was less doctrinaire than his parishioner; the disgruntled Bobby had to report that the answer was, "It all depends." This hot-headed and narrowminded Bobby Kennedy gave no hint of the stature he would eventually achieve.

Yet Anatoly Dobrynin, whose meetings with Bobby were crucial to the resolution of the Cuban Missile Crisis, seems to have recognized the man I knew. In his message to Khrushchev he described Bobby's final proposal: get the missiles out of Cuba and the president will secretly agree to take American missiles out of Turkey. Trying to impress Khrushchev with the seriousness of Bobby's proposal, Dobrynin wrote, "He didn't even try to get into fights on various subjects as he usually does." The Bobby we knew was changing.

Still, his obstinate moral intuitions may have been a virtue in this crisis. In his mind, the United States picking on Cuba was like a big guy picking on a little guy. He was not prepared to give up moral convictions in the face of technical expertise. The best line in the film is given to JFK, but it also applies to Bobby: "There is something immoral about abandoning your own judgment."

Bobby continued to grow as a man after his brother's assassination, but at the core he still saw himself as an underdog, able to identify with all the underdogs and they with him. But the film fails to develop Bobby's character, and focuses instead on Kevin Costner's Kenny O'Donnell.

Like Bobby Kennedy, Kenny O'Donnell seemed an unlikely football player. Kenny came to Harvard after serving during World War II. He had been a bombardier, and received a purple heart and several medals for the many flights he had flown over Europe. He was even smaller than Bobby and looked like he might be blown away by the next strong breeze. But he was an uncanny pass defender, the best on the team, and his interceptions often kept our losing Harvard team in the game. Even in practice he was prepared to do anything it took to win. He was a master at concealing the illegal holding he used routinely to get an edge on bigger players.

No one got angry with this leprechaun; in fact, we all respected him and feared his withering sardonic wit. It was Kenny, our captain in 1948, who scored the winning touchdown against Yale while playing on a broken leg. But Kenny was not a happy hero. There was an air of desolation, a missing vitality. Even then he was drinking too much—a struggle that continued throughout his life.

The friendship between Bobby and Kenny was like the prince and the pauper, each envying what the other seemed to have. At the same time, their friendship was a paradigm of the

Kennedy family's political alliance. Jack would build his political organization by reaching out to World War II veterans, especially working-class Catholics, for whom the Kennedys were royalty. It was Rose, the queen mother and daughter of Boston's legendary mayor, who knew and could rub shoulders with that constituency. And it was Bobby, the shy prince, who had to reach out to the campaign workers. Bobby's friendship with Kenny and the other returning veterans on the football team was the crucial experience he needed for his role as Jack's campaign manager. Bobby felt comfortable bantering with Kenny. They were psychologically similar: overshadowed younger brothers, Irish, believing Catholics, obsessed with throwing and catching a football, and unimpressed with anyone who claimed to be better than they were.

Kenny's official Kennedy career began in 1952, when Bobby, who was managing Jack's campaign to unseat Henry Cabot Lodge Jr.

in the U.S. Senate, prevailed upon Kenny to work on the campaign. Kenny dropped out of Boston College Law School, which he hated, and never looked back. After Jack won the election, Kenny worked full-time for the Kennedys; when there wasn't a political campaign, Joseph Kennedy gave him a job. Eight short years later Bobby Kennedy took his "Irish Mafia" (several from that Harvard football team) to Washington—they had elected the first Catholic president, and now Kenny O'Donnell stood guard at the White House as JFK's appointment secretary. He had a new nickname, "Cobra," and his loyalty to the Kennedys was absolute.

It seems to me that the high point in Kenny's service to the Kennedys can be found in his testimony to the Warren Commission. JFK's corpse lay in a room in the Parkland Hospital in Dallas. The Texas authorities were determined under their laws to do a local autopsy. Jackie Kennedy would not leave the president's body; she wanted to take her dead husband back to

Washington. With help from a Secret Service agent, Kenny hustled the president's body out of the hospital past the protesting officials into an ambulance and told the driver not to stop until they were on Air Force One. That is the man I knew. Jackie Kennedy never forgot: she paid for Kenny's funeral.

Kenny O'Donnell's life, or at least his purpose in life, came to an end with the assassination of the Kennedy brothers. His daughter says he died of a broken heart and the Irish cancer—alcoholism. Now Kevin Costner has made him larger in death than he ever was in life.

Ironically, the only person who ever credited Kenny with playing such a crucial role in the Cuban Missile Crisis was his good friend Bobby Kennedy. After JFK's death, Kenny O'Donnell came back to Massachusetts and ran for governor. He was a terrible candidate—he could not bear the humiliation of asking people to vote for him. The only bright spot in his desultory campaign was when his friend

Bobby came and made a speech on his behalf. Without batting an eyelash Bobby assured the audience that "During the Cuban Missile Crisis [Kenny] was one of the two or three major advisers to President Kennedy." *Thirteen Days* turns Bobby's political white lie into historical reality and gives world-saving powers to the friendship I witnessed taking shape.

Moment of Grace

Thirteen Conversations About One Thing, 2002

THIRTEEN CONVERSATIONS ABOUT ONE *Thing* is the second film by the Sprecher sisters (their first was *Clockwatchers*), who are a refreshing presence in the egomaniacal world of moviemaking. Jill Sprecher is a shy and self-effacing director who hands out credit to everyone else. Now in her 40s, she continues to be animated by philosophical questions about transience, contingency, and the meaning of life that puzzled her in college. Karen Sprecher, who coauthored the screenplays with her older sister, is trained as a psychiatric social worker and gives the characters who ponder these questions in *Thirteen Conversations* psychological depth.

Perhaps because the sisters and *Thirteen Conversations* break the Hollywood mold, critics have tried to locate their work in relation to other filmmakers. Those who like it find echoes of Woody Allen, Ingmar Bergman, Krzysztof Kieslowski, and Robert Altman. Those who don't like it see outtakes from Stanley Kubrick's *Eyes Wide Shut* and a rip-off of Paul Thomas Anderson's *Magnolia*. What runs through the work of this disparate collection of filmmakers is an interest in the dark side of the psyche—where people (all of us) question life's meaning and worry that it has none. How you find happiness after you ask yourself that question is one of the subjects of this unusual film.

Neither the plot nor timeline of *Thirteen Conversations* is linear. Several stories are told, linked by coincidence, and the sequence of 13 segments that make up the film circle like a Möbius strip.

John Turturro plays a college physics professor whose rule-ridden rigidity keeps life at a distance. He seems to know this in the way a patient can correctly describe his problem to his psychoanalyst without ever really getting it. Every attempt to break out of his prison simply narrows the space between the bars.

When we first meet him he is having dinner with his wife (Amy Irving). Although they still go through the motions of marriage, neither has anything left for the other except veiled resentment. Only later do we understand that he is having an affair and that she, unbeknownst to him, has found out. He was recently mugged and pistol-whipped, and when his discarded wallet was returned she found evidence of the affair. Instead of confronting him, she asks him why he is not angry or upset about the mugging. He, with a physicist's objectivity, allows that the incident shook him from his routine. But it is obvious from every bite of asparagus that he is unshakable. His wife despairingly asks, "What is it that you want?" and he answers, "What everyone wants: to experience life, to wake up enthused, to be happy." No real person, not even a physicist, talks this way. But if the lines are not realistic in any sociocultural sense they are certainly true to Turturro's narcissistic character and to the part of us that identifies with him. And the Sprechers are interested in that truth: their film is an examination of how the self suffers and survives.

Jill Sprecher has told her personal story of trauma and survival in several interviews. While walking near the Port Authority Bus Terminal in New York, she was clubbed over the head in an apparently random attack. She needed emergency brain surgery and took months to recover from her injuries. This counts as psychic trauma in anyone's book, but she was able to forgive her mentally ill attacker. A few weeks later someone close to her "did something really small that just cut me like a knife," and she has carried the scar of that painful moment for years. Sprecher realizes that psychic trauma is not objectively quantifiable but can only be understood in terms of its subjective meaning as a personal crisis. One will not find this insight in modern textbooks of psychiatry. But surely Sprecher is right, and she has played out that idea in several of the characters in her film.

The Sprechers are also interested in what may be the most fundamental question in human psychology: What is it that actually changes a person? One can ask that question in the consulting room or in daily life. And it is not just a question for the psychotherapist. It is this spiritual question William James tried to answer in his classic *Varieties of Religious Experience*. James's book is less a philosophical analysis of religious experience than a collection of personal accounts of life-changing encounters with faith. So *Thirteen Conversations*, in its understated way, offers a fundamental psychological and spiritual inquiry into the human condition.

The physics professor, like Jill Sprecher, has been mugged but has suffered no psychic injury; his trauma, like hers, will come in a more intimate way. The brief dinner scene is the first of the vignettes, all set in New York City. The next scene features Matthew McConaughey as a young assistant district attorney, Troy, who is in a Manhattan saloon celebrating a successful prosecution with some of his colleagues. Troy is on top of his world, professionally successful and at the same time doing something right and useful for society—punishing the guilty. At the bar he encounters a seeming misanthrope (Alan Arkin) who begrudges the young lawyer his happiness and sense of accomplishment. Driving home, Troy accidentally (perhaps he had too much to drink) hits a young woman on a deserted street in the Village. He gets out of his BMW, looks at what he thinks is her dead body, and leaves the scene of the crime. Secret guilt begins to torment him. A small cut on his forehead, sustained in the accident, mysteriously does not heal. Later we will see that he is using a razor blade to keep his wound from healing. His black-and-white world collapses into shades of gray when he interviews a murderer. As the young criminal describes the radically contingent circumstances that led up to the killing, Troy realizes that "there but for the grace of God go I." Troy will eventually be driven to attempt suicide; indeed the possibility of suicide—the death of the self—haunts the film.

In subsequent vignettes we learn that Troy's hit-and-run victim is the angelic, unassuming, generous Beatrice (Clea DuVall), who is the Sprecher "self" in the film. She and her jaded girlfriend work for a cleaning service; Beatrice cheerfully does all the work while her friend slacks off. Beatrice, who sings Bach in a church choir, has faith that good things happen, while her lazy friend tells her that the world isn't fair. Like Jill Sprecher, Beatrice requires emergency brain surgery, yet she survives and maintains her faith in benevolent providence. Then comes a small cutting remark that causes her personal crisis. One of Beatrice's jobs is cleaning the apartment of an architect, and she has a crush on him that she wishfully thinks he reciprocates. When she goes to the architect's apartment after her recovery to return a shirt she had promised to mend, he inadvertently reveals that he had thought she had stolen his watch. That he would have such a thought destroys her dream and her faith in the goodness of life. Like Troy she is on the edge of suicide; their lives and their "happy" outlooks have been changed in an instant. Both will get a second chance.

Unlike them, a middle-management insurance claims adjuster named Gene (Alan Arkin) has already learned to expect the worst from life. When he first appears at the saloon, he announces his distrust of happiness: "Show me a happy man," he says, "and I'll show you a disaster waiting to happen" (another fortune-cookie line). Arkin gives a virtuoso performance as the bitter, hardworking New Yorker, tormented by an employee who is relentlessly cheerful, proud of his children (Gene's son is a drug addict), and always smiling. Gene treats him cruelly, but in the end it is he who surprises us with his heart of gold, or at least his conscience. Like William James and the Sprechers, Gene wonders if it is possible to change one's life for the better. He remembers leaving home to attend a career-training program near the end of his marriage. He and his wife were not getting along, and he happened to see her standing at the window watching him leave. What, he wonders, would have happened if he had waved at her instead of walking away? Might his entire life have been different?

Thirteen Conversations is partly about the loneliness and alienation of its characters. For some, there is no hope: Turturro's professor is eventually forced to confront himself. His lover delivers the ultimate indictment as she ends their affair. Her husband has found out about them and has told her he cannot live without her. "What, compared to that, can you say?" she asks Turturro. The stricken look on his face tells us that the narcissist has no answer and never will. Other characters, however, are saved. As the Sprechers' characters circle around the question of what to expect from life and each other, we glimpse an answer: momentary redemption through an act of grace.

Troy survives a suicide attempt, learns that the woman he ran over survived and that he can make amends. The suicidal Beatrice who is now ready to step intentionally in front of an oncoming car picks out a man across the street to focus her resolve. She catches his eye and then quite unexpectedly—"he must have read my mind"—the man smiles at her, spontaneously restoring her faith in benevolent providence. The Sprechers juxtapose Beatrice's story with a shot of Gene's always-smiling employee walking along the sidewalk. Surely if he was the man he did not read her mind; he smiles at everyone, annoying some but perhaps saving

Beatrice. The mystery of grace in the Sprech-ers' film is captured in these moments that are entirely contingent and perhaps unreal, and yet in such moments human beings can find hope and meaning in their lives.

Thirteen Conversations feels like a miracle. The acting is superb, the editing is inspired, the noirish cinematography resonates with the oneiric mood. And if the characters are not realistic, they are worth believing in. The true measure of the Sprechers' achievement is that some of us will leave the theater convinced, at least for the moment, of the possibility of grace.

Holy War
The Battle of Algiers, 1966

"PEOPLE PRACTICALLY NEVER EXPERIENCE the great events of history with their own eyes," explained the Italian filmmaker Gillo Pontecorvo; they experience them only through the "200 mm or 300 mm lens" of the mass media. Applying this insight, Pontecorvo captured one of the most important anti-imperial conflicts of the 20th century by filming *The Battle of Algiers* in black and white, using lenses and camera angles to simulate that era's newsreels. Pontecorvo succeeded so well that many viewers thought they had watched a documentary about the revolutionary struggle of the Algerian National Liberation Front (FLN) against their French colonial oppressors.

Pontecorvo succeeded on a political level as well: he convinced middle-class audiences that terrorism—deliberately bombing innocent people in order to pressure political opponents—might be necessary. His case was so emotionally compelling that Pauline Kael described *The Battle of Algiers* as "the rape of the doubting intelligence." She dubbed Pontecorvo the most dangerous kind of Marxist: a "Marxist poet" who uses the power of film to persuade his audience that "terrorism is a tragic necessity."

The Battle of Algiers was the first European political film of the left. Pontecorvo wanted to portray the Marxist understanding of history as an inevitable process that "once begun cannot be stopped." In the film, when the leader of the FLN—played by the actual leader of the FLN—is captured and the French paratroopers seem to have broken the back of the secret revolutionary organization, he is paraded before a press conference and asked if the FLN is now defeated. "In my opinion," he replies, "the NLF [FLN] has more chances of beating the French Army than the French have of stopping history." Pontecorvo, a committed Marxist, commented on that line. "Not only did we believe this to be right, but we really liked the idea it was right." History was moving "in a certain way," and the class struggle would continue in the Third World with colonized peoples taking up arms against the colonizers. It was Frantz Fanon's psychiatric gloss on Marxism, endorsed by Sartre. The wretched of the earth, the black faces condemned to wear white masks, would assert their identity through acts of violence and rise up against oppression even when it came from "super-civilized France." The French had been defeated by that march of history in Vietnam, and Pontecorvo wanted to depict the last futile stand of the French colonial empire in Algiers. Pontecorvo claimed his filmmaking was ruled by the "Dictatorship of Truth," and his version of Truth certainly disturbed the French, who banned his film. Certainly many critics saw in *The Battle of Algiers* the power of truth revealed. Others—most prominently Kael—saw not truth but ultimate propaganda. *The Battle of Algiers*, she said, "ranks with" *Triumph of the Will*, Leni Riefenstahl's deification of Hitler. Whether revealed truth or ultimate propaganda, *The Battle of Algiers* is a text that might give Americans some perspective on our own situation after 9/11—both through its official message and through its unintended insights.

Kael was not wrong when she described Pontecorvo as a Marxist poet, but he meant his poetry as a celebration of humanity. He described himself as "someone who approached man and the human condition with a feeling of warmth and compassion." His film and his poetry were an attempt to connect himself and his Western audiences through their common humanity to Arabs of the Casbah. He embraced what is different about the Arabs, including their Islamic traditions, and made them fully human to us. Yes, revolutionary terror is a tragic necessity. But Pontecorvo's inspiration is utopian. Revolution held for him the promise of community and comradeship. He made his audience share that feeling of community so that we might accept the possibility of justified terrorism.

After 9/11 the moral imagination of most Americans could not conceive of a Pontecorvo-style justification for such acts of terrorism. President Bush spoke for the passionate convictions of the American public when he promised retribution. Overnight, many leftist doves turned into war hawks. Something had to be done, and it seemed more than reasonable to invade an Afghanistan ruled by the Taliban, who were cruel to women, sheltered Osama Bin Laden, and hated Americans.

Since 9/11 we have been following a Pontecorvo script: threatened by Muslim terrorists as the French were in Algeria, we have been caught up in a spontaneous burst of patriotic solidarity. More than a year later we congratulate ourselves for doing in months what the Soviet Union failed to accomplish in years in Afghanistan, and the march to war continues as President Bush perseveres in what is now called "Operation Enduring Freedom."

Pontecorvo's film is perhaps most ironically instructive on that American rallying cry. Ignoring all legal restraints and using torture to gain the information necessary to destroy the FLN, French paratroopers win the Battle of Algiers, but as we are shown, they lose the war for the French colonial empire. Without warning, two years after the French victory, the entire Arab population swarms out of the Casbah to march on Algiers. The French respond with every brutal technique of riot control at their disposal—gas, machine guns, and tanks—to drive the Arabs back. Then, as night and fog fall over the city, a French police authority addresses the invisible mob through a megaphone. "What do you want?" he asks in bewilderment. In response, Arabs emerge from the fog demanding and celebrating *their* freedom. Pontecorvo had imagined this scene as an ecstatic ballet, the camera focused on an Arab woman pushed down again and again by the French police; each time, she rises up in a dance of freedom. This was the revelation to Western audiences: the Muslims of the Casbah were freedom fighters.

In her 1972 review, Kael wrote that Pontecorvo's historical-determinist film showed us how "the Algerian people were spontaneously turned into Marxist revolutionaries by historical events." But *The Battle of Algiers* conveys another message that was lost on contemporary audiences, and apparently on Pontecorvo himself. Watching the film recently for the first time in many years, I saw that Pontecorvo had achieved something beyond his conscious artistic and political intentions. Like Tolstoy, who wanted to show the evils of adultery in

Anna Karenina but created a character that transcended his moralistic agenda, Pontecorvo's Algerians transcend Marxist categories. The historical turn is to traditional Islam, not enlightenment progress. If Pontecorvo could now revisit his own film, he might recognize—as we can with the hindsight of 9/11—the essential place of Islam in the film's setting and how that background context has now become its central message.

To appreciate this other message one must look past the original script (which has been published) and consider what Pontecorvo put into his finished product. With his writer Franco Solinas, Pontecorvo created a screenplay out of a Marxist-Fanonian screed, and that is what the audiences saw at the time. Yet what he filmed shows how important Arab-Muslim fundamentalist identity was for the mobilization of the people of the Casbah. The very first FLN communiqué to the people of Algiers in the film (not in the published screenplay) proclaims, "Our revolt is against colonialism, our goal to restore independent Algeria within *the framework of Islamic principles* with respect for the basic freedoms regardless of race or religion." And throughout *The Battle of Algiers*, Islam, not Marxism, provides the yeast of the revolutionary solidarity. The film portrays a cleansing of the Arab peoples by a return to Islamic principles and to a puritanical Islam that blames the French colonizers for imposing European decadence on Algiers. It is the French who have made the Arabs their prostitutes, undermined the traditional authority of the Muslim family, brought cigarette smoking, alcoholism, and drugs to their community.

The FLN begins its campaign not by teaching Marxism but by preaching Islam. The FLN understands that its recruits are marginalized outcasts with every reason to hate the French and with nothing to lose. Both these recruits, and the Arabs of the Casbah, must be purified before they can undertake guerilla warfare; that purification will come through a return to Islamic traditions, and through violence in the name of Islam. Pontecorvo's central example of this process is the young Arab, Ali La Pointe, an illiterate juvenile, sometime boxer, grifter, and street criminal. He is ready to join the FLN after he witnesses from his prison window the guillotining of a man who goes to his death chanting "*Tahia el Djezair*" (Long live Algeria). To join the revolutionary underground Ali must agree to kill a French policeman. The FLN trick him with an unloaded gun: this test is only to prove that he is not a French double agent. His real rite of passage into the FLN will come when he kills a friend, an Arab pimp who controls a string of brothels.

All this is now so obvious and undeniable, it seems strange that even the clear-eyed Pauline Kael could not see it. What might be even more astonishing is the suggestion that Pontecorvo created all this without appreciating what he was doing.

How did so much Islamic fundamentalism find its way into Pontecorvo's film? The explanation lies in the way the film was made. Yacef Saadi, who had been the military head of the FLN in Algiers, came to Italy looking for a director to make a movie of the Algerian struggle from the Algerian point of view. Pontecorvo was third on the list, and was chosen only after the first two declined. The Algerians could not provide much money, but they could give the filmmaker access to any site he wanted and put crowds of people at his disposal. And he made good use of what he was given. Crowds became the protagonists of the film. Pontecorvo had been a journalist and a still photographer, and he decided—with one notable exception—not to use professional actors.

With a photographer's eye Pontecorvo chose people whose faces are visually arresting; the actors, at least in appearance, are authentic. But such actors could not be expected to give convincing expression to Marxist slogans.

Pontecorvo's one prominent professional actor, Jean Martin, plays Colonel Mathieu, who had fought in Vietnam and is sympathetic with the liberation movement. He is given all the polemical lines about Marxism; that frees the Algerians to speak and to act out their own Arab-Islamic identity. So Pontecorvo gave them lines natural to them, the product of long interviews with FLN members and Algerians who had participated in the events depicted. One could almost say Pontecorvo psychoanalyzed the participants and distilled their collective memories into his dialogue.

As Pontecorvo began to film and edit, he continually added touches to convey the particulars of Algerian life in the Casbah. His impulse was to convey "the feelings and the emotions shared by a multitude." What his Algerian actors and extras shared was their Islamic tradition. In the final scene where the Algerians appear out of the night and fog and demand their freedom, Pontecorvo had originally intended to have all the extras chanting political slogans, but later he decided it did not work artistically. Then he hit on the idea of having the Arab women erupt into their traditional ululation—rhythmic piercing cries. It has a powerful effect, but the effect is of the unifying claim of Arab identity rather than of the brotherhood of revolution. Pontecorvo thought it worked so well that he used it in an earlier moment of the film as the rallying cry of the Casbah.

At another crucial moment, a French police supervisor—in an unofficial act of counterterrorism—sets off dynamite in the Casbah, destroying homes and killing innocent people. In the explosion's wake, three Arab women are shown cutting their hair and putting on make-up and French-style dress. There can be no doubt that this is a ritual moment of Western degradation as these modest Muslim women are being transformed into sexual objects. And as they deliver their retaliation—hidden time bombs—some French soldiers and other men hit on them. Each woman looks around the crowded places that their bombs will destroy. One woman's gaze lingers on a small boy licking his ice-cream cone—and then she leaves her bomb. Each fully appreciates that there will be innocent victims. Watching them today, it seems clear that Islamic faith, not revolutionary solidarity, made their mission sacred.

Pontecorvo thought that the French torture of their captives was worse than any Algerian terrorism, but his artistry now also reveals the holy-war horror of the Casbah uprising against the decadent west. As America rallies behind President Bush's crusade against the axis of evil, there is more horror to come. If you have a "doubting intelligence," it is time to look at the lessons of history revealed in Pontecorvo's *The Battle of Algiers* and think for yourself.

The Content of
Our Character

The Station Agent, 2003

HOLLYWOOD USUALLY RELEGATES DWARFS
to fantasy-world caricatures, cheerful gro-
tesques, most famously the Munchkins in *The
Wizard of Oz*. Given Hollywood's current en-
thusiasm for imaginary realms, dwarfs willing
to play these roles have lots of work. But Peter
Dinklage, the star of *The Station Agent*, has
always refused to be stereotyped.

The Station Agent didn't start out as a film
about a dwarf. The aspiring filmmaker Tom
McCarthy had been working on a screenplay
that he hoped would become his first film when
he suddenly had the idea of casting Dinklage,
who he had directed on stage, as his leading
man. Enlisting Dinklage's help, he rewrote the

screenplay, incorporating Dinklage's accounts of his own experiences and making them central. In the early scenes of *The Station Agent*, it is obviously McCarthy's intention to have Dinklage's size—he is four feet six inches tall—affect the audience as well as his fellow characters. But as the movie unfolds it is the actor's understated performance, his personal dignity, and his handsome face to which one is drawn.

I cannot claim to have immediately appreciated what McCarthy and Dinklage—the collaboration should be emphasized—had achieved in their quirky film. The first time I saw *The Station Agent* I was prepared to dismiss it as sentimental pandering to political correctness. The good guys were the dwarf, Fin; a Cuban, Joe (Bobby Cannavale); an African-American girl, Cleo (Raven Goodwin); and a woman on the verge of a nervous breakdown, Olivia (Patricia Clarkson). The bad guys were rude and insensitive white men. But *The Station Agent* stayed with me, perhaps because of its quirks, and I began to recognize its psychologically nuanced power—and, most importantly, I understood that McCarthy had never condescended to nor exploited Dinklage.

The inescapable questions of *The Station Agent*—and of Dinklage's life—are how will people respond to his dwarfism, and how will he react to their gawking, head-turning, wisecracks, and occasional cruelty? Each person's reaction reveals something psychologically significant about him or her, and Dinklage's response defines his psychological identity.

Dinklage has the defiant nobility of the court dwarfs captured by the 17th-century Spanish painter Velázquez. Look carefully and you will see that he depicts them as equal human beings to the Spanish nobility who are his usual subjects. But such is the elemental power of the film medium that it can have greater impact than the genius of Velázquez. Film can compel empathy. It can lift audiences out of their settled convictions and let them glimpse something of themselves in the alien other. Mc-Carthy has used that power so that we will see in Dinklage not just a "short-limbed dwarf" but an everyman in a morality play of face-to-face encounters with other human beings.

Erving Goffman made us recognize the importance of what he called "the presentation of self in everyday life." All of us know what it feels like to be slighted in public, to be the center of unwanted attention, to worry that people are whispering about us and laughing at us. And some of us know, or at least sense, the cruelty in the derogatory reactions to the shamed victim. We can only imagine, and films like *The Station Agent* help us to imagine, what face-to-face encounters are like for people stigmatized by nature. McCarthy's film is a meditation on how Finbar McBride, a proud man, comes to terms with the humiliation of face-to-face encounters—a domain in which psychology and morality are inextricably linked in the challenge of treating the other as an equal human being. McCarthy's film goes deeper, exploring grief, loneliness, and the impulse to find a utopia in solitude or at least a haven from the heartless world of others.

When we first meet Fin he seems to have found that haven. He works for Henry Styles (Paul Benjamin), the African-American owner of a model-train store in Hoboken, New Jersey. Both are alone except for each other, their shared interest in trains, and their mutual respect and understanding. When Henry dies suddenly, Finbar is left unemployed, with no one and nothing but an abandoned train station in the boondocks of Newfoundland, New Jersey, that Henry has bequeathed to him.

How Fin gets to Newfoundland is never clear. We see him walking next to the tracks as trains thunder by, and walking on the tracks until he arrives at his desolate station. Has he walked all the way from Hoboken? We can't know, but these images establish Fin's total pre-occupation—his obsession—with trains as the mark of his isolation. There must have been a remarkable working relationship between director McCarthy, cinematographer Oliver Bokelberg, and film editor Tom McArdle. Operating on a small budget, they decided to use their resources to explore the felt experience of the characters rather than lay out every step of the narrative. The man juxtaposed with the trains is an important and recurring cinematographic theme. In one scene Fin will stand on top of an abandoned train—a lonely little man carefully positioned toward one end of the top of the passenger car. The image is arresting. Like much of the cinematography in *The Station Agent*, this scene has all the force of a still photograph. Similar moments hold the film together and show us how the team used Dinklage's size to create powerful images that challenge viewers' voyeurism or simple pity.

Once in Newfoundland, Fin, an orderly chain-smoker in a black suit and white shirt, structures his solitude with routines. Fin is grieving for Henry, but we also sense that he does not expect to find another such like-minded friend. He wants most of all to be left alone. Solitude is to be his anodyne. Indifference to others is to be his studied defense. His psychological armor will make him seem stronger and more self-sufficient than the people he will meet in Newfoundland.

I have no knowledge of what McCarthy's screenplay looked like before he hit on the idea of casting Dinklage. But I suspect it may have been premised on a character much like the one Dustin Hoffman played in the Oscar-winning film *Rain Man*. Finbar's preoccupation with trains goes beyond a hobby or avocation. Psychologically, his obsession resembles the fixed interest of the idiot-savant form of autism. For reasons not yet understood, idiot savants like the Rain Man character are not capable of emotional development. Their inability to share the human emotions that connect us is tragic; opting for Fin instead created the possibility that the character might develop emotionally, and also the opportunity for us to understand Fin's obsession not as a peculiar limitation of mind but as a monastic vocation—an anchorite's retreat from the cruelty of others.

If Fin wants isolation, it turns out that he has come to the wrong place. In another gap in the narrative logic of the screenplay, a catering truck sits in the parking lot of the empty train station. But emotions move this film along, and Joe Oramas, the driver (filling in for his sick father), belongs there because he is an extroverted man desperate for company. Joe, like everyone else Fin meets, first reacts only to his size. But his own loneliness, his conviviality, and his insatiable curiosity quickly lead him to try to befriend Fin. He will even become interested in trains. Cannavale's character—both innocent and raunchy—brings most of the humor to the film.

Fin soon encounters other inhabitants of Newfoundland, most significantly Olivia, who is so flustered when she catches sight of him on the road that she nearly runs him over. Clarkson was awarded a Special Jury Prize for Outstanding Performance at Sundance for her Olivia, and I might have appreciated her more had I not seen her recently in *Pieces of April*, where she also plays an overwrought woman near breakdown. In *The Station Agent* she is the emotional antithesis of Fin. Her only child, a boy, died in a playground fall during a moment of inattention. She is filled with grief and guilt. Like Fin, she has retreated from others, in her case to the solitude of her summer home, where she is trying to paint.

After nearly running over Fin twice in one day, she brings a bottle of whiskey to his apartment in the station as an apology. When she gets drunk and falls asleep and Joe sees her emerge the next morning, he assumes the obvious and suggests a threesome. Joe's estimation of Fin's sexual prowess becomes further inflated when a dipsy young librarian named

Emily (Michelle Williams) spends the night in the station. In truth, Fin wants nothing from these women and offers nothing but his usual respectful demeanor. And rather than sleeping with Fin, both women begin to confide in him. Olivia eventually tells him about her loss and her fear that she can have no more children. And Emily, who has told no one else, confesses to him that she is pregnant. Is it because Fin is a dwarf, or does his willed emotional detachment, like a psychoanalyst's professional demeanor, allow them to reveal themselves?

Fin's wall of reserve begins to melt in the warmth of Joe's determined charm and his growing feelings for Olivia. Along the way, little Cleo has broken through as well. She gets off to an awkward start when she asks him innocently what grade he's in, and then, "Are you a midget?" Fin good-naturedly explains that he is a dwarf. Cleo's candid questions are without malice or mockery; she, like him, seems to be a loner interested in trains.

With these friends Fin has begun to make a life in Newfoundland, but there is still the problem of the larger community's reaction to his dwarfism. In the only moment of bathos in the film, Fin goes to the local bar and gets drunk after letting down his defenses with Olivia and being rejected. At the bar Fin's detachment gives way to angry defiance at the gawking strangers. The camera makes him look grotesque—a huge head on a tiny body—as he climbs on top of his barstool and shouts to everyone who has been eyeing him, "Take a good look."

Several movie reviewers found fault with this scene, as though Fin's humiliation was out of keeping with the rest of the film. But to me it seems crucial to the psychological development of Fin's character and to the film's project. Fin staggers out of the bar and collapses on the train tracks as one of his beloved trains roars down on him. He gives a ghastly smile of welcome to his annihilation. But morning comes and he is alive. Was the train a dream? Then he notices that the precious pocket watch he used to time the trains has been crushed. Was he saved by a miracle? Be it dream or miracle, Fin, as every man in this morality play of the human encounter, has faced up to his worst fears of humiliation and the possibility of his own death. He has survived, and he has changed.

Later, when Cleo asks him to come to school and talk to her class about trains, he first declines, explaining that he would have to face the reflexive cruelty of children. Cleo, wise beyond her years, tells him that if he cares about her he can and will come. Fin shows up in Cleo's class and endures the cruelty he anticipated. But he is also asked a surprising question by one of the children: Why trains? What about zeppelins?

Fin does not find love at the end of this film, but he has let down the barriers that protected him from being wounded by others. In the last scene Joe, Olivia, and he seem to be enjoying a newfound friendship, and Fin is secure enough to repeat the question: "What about zeppelins?!"

The Station Agent is a charming film that reminds us that, be they kind or nasty, other people are our only possibility of happiness.

The End of Remorse

The Passion of the Christ, 2004

MOST PEOPLE I TALK TO ARE BOYCOTTING *The Passion of the Christ*. They have been convinced that the film is dangerously anti-Semitic and that it would be an act of betrayal to contribute to its commercial success. They assume that my reason for going was to weigh in with another denunciation of Mel Gibson—the film's writer and director—and his Holocaust-denying father.

In fact I decided to see and review the film for three very different reasons. First, *The Passion* is one of the rare movies that is also an important cultural event—a significant historical moment. My friends may be boycotting it, but audiences across America and around the world are attending in record numbers, and many Christians are coming away with a sense of restored faith. It seems to me a mistake to turn one's back on a cultural event of this magnitude.

Second, I hoped to understand the deeply contradictory reactions to the film by intelligent people of good will. Writing in *The New Republic*, Leon Wieseltier denounced the small-minded Gibson and his sacred "snuff film"— soaked in blood, reveling in torture, and resurrecting anti-Semitism as religious dogma. Wieseltier, the child of Holocaust survivors, bitterly complained that Gibson's literal reading of the Gospels omitted Christ's most important message: love and forgiveness. But a distinguished Catholic colleague confided to me that she had wept through the scenes of Christ's flagellation and crucifixion. She came away from the film with a deeper sense of Christ's suffering and felt regret that she had not been a better Christian. She assured me the film was not anti-Semitic and sent me a review from the interreligious journal *First Things* that described *The Passion* as "the best movie ever made about Jesus Christ" while confidently denying any "concerns about the film stirring up anti-Judaism."

Finally, many of the greatest filmmakers have wanted to do a version of the Christ story. It is perhaps the most important story of Western civilization, and film is the most powerful medium our civilization has invented for storytelling. But how do you translate a sacred text into a screenplay? Pier Paolo Pasolini did a Marxist version, Franco Zeffirelli did a Sunday-school documentary, and Martin Scorsese used Nikos Kazantzakis's existential novel, a book on the Catholic Index of Prohibited Books, to make *The Last Temptation of Christ*, a remarkable but anti-Church telling of the story. Gibson, who found religion as he struggled with alcoholism and suicidal depression, wanted to portray the Catholic faith that saved him.

He describes his filmmaking as—and I believe him—an act of faith.

As I waited in line to enter the theater, an elderly woman who was coming out stopped to advise me that I would need two handkerchiefs. She was wrong: I sat dry-eyed, stunned, and with a growing sense of dread as I watched what was for me the most anti-Semitic film I had ever seen in my life. Even more horrifying was the realization that I could not dismiss *The Passion* as a second-rate film. All of the snide put-downs of Gibson's filmmaking are in my view unjustified. Yes, one can connect the dots from the torture scenes of *Mad Max* to *Lethal Weapon* to *Braveheart* to *The Passion*, but Gibson is a serious person who has created a powerful film. The cinematography is an astonishing accomplishment inspired by great religious art. It is also the most cruel and bloody I have ever seen. Episodes of sadistic brutality establish the rhythm of the film, taking the audience again and again to the limits of its capacity to endure its bloody vision of Christ's suffering. Yet neither I nor anyone else in that crowded, hushed theater walked out.

Lines from Isaiah 53:5, familiar from Handel's *Messiah*, preface the film: "He was wounded for our transgressions." In the Bible, this follows the more famous lines of Isaiah 53:3: "He is despised and rejected of men; a man of sorrows, and acquainted with grief." Surprisingly, the quotation is accompanied by a specific date (742 B.C.): in other words, this suffering was prophesied, and it came to pass. This is serious religiosity. Through a blue haze we discern Jesus (James Caviezel) praying in the Garden of Gethsemane. Caviezel is not asked or allowed to act the part of Jesus; he exists only as the human body in which the Christ is incarnate and will suffer. For that purpose he is superbly cast. Gibson wanted his cinematography to pay homage to Caravaggio, and Caviezel's body is very much like Jesus' in the great painter's *Flagellation of Christ*.

But on Caravaggio's canvas Christ's body is entirely unmarked. While Gibson's film may have started with Caravaggio, it ends with the tortured, flayed Christ of the Northern Renaissance. From the first moment we see Jesus he is in agony, praying to God and wrestling with the temptations of an androgynous Satan, played by a woman with a shaved skull (Rosalinda Celentano). We will witness Jesus' betrayal by Judas and see him taken in chains to the high priests of the temple. If there is a false note in Gibson's depiction, it is sounded almost at once, as his Christ is surrounded by sadists, be they Jews or Romans, who take malicious pleasure in inflicting pain. The temple guards cudgel him even before he has been judged. Then the Roman soldiers exhaust themselves in the brutal pleasure of whipping and scourging the "King of the Jews." Christ is not only made to suffer beyond human endurance, but under Gibson's direction he refuses to surrender to the pain and loss of blood. Incredibly, he struggles to his feet, only to incite the Roman soldiers to beat him down again with greater violence, using more vicious instruments that tear away flesh. Yes, this is prototypical Gibson-macho, but it is also a compelling depiction of the sacred spirit, incarnate and refusing to succumb. The torture is sustained for most of the film until it reaches its apogee on the cross as Christ asks why he has been forsaken. All this is precisely as Gibson intended. His purpose was to make Christ's suffering visible—Christ, who suffered for the sins of mankind.

What one sees in this protracted torture depends on whether you came into the theater believing in Christ. Without that faith one might see, as Wieseltier did, only Gibson's proclivity for sadomasochism. Yet Roger Ebert, a onetime altar boy who participated in many Lenten and Easter services, described his quite different experience of the very same scenes: "What Gibson has provided for me, for the first time in my life, is a visceral idea of what the Passion consisted of." Ebert's report is remarkable, and, for me, entirely believable. We have no more powerful demonstration of the axiom that everyone in a theater sees a different film.

I thought about how my experiences had determined the frightening anti-Semitism that I saw. What immediately came to mind was my best friend telling me—we were both eight years old at the time—that he had been taught by his priest that "you Jews killed Jesus." I had no idea what response to make to that accusation or even whether I should tell my parents about it. If you see *The Passion* through that lens, I think you too will be horrified.

Other alarms went off in my head. The high priests look and behave like all the familiar anti-Semitic stereotypes—the selfish, obstinate, unforgiving Jews one tries to look past in the great religious paintings. They cannot be ignored when Gibson brings them to life on the screen. Wieseltier was particularly incensed that Gibson had told Diane Sawyer on television, "Critics who have a problem with me don't really have a problem with me and this film. They have a problem with the four Gospels." Gibson has, I fear, a much better argument than Wieseltier allows. It is very difficult to find a scene in *The Passion* that is not in Matthew, Mark, Luke, or John. Gibson has placed his filmmaking gloss on the text, but with great fidelity to its words. And although the Vatican has now denied that the Pope pronounced after he saw the film, "It is as it was," he might well have said that. The Pope saw the film that many Catholics are seeing, the one in which the Son of God suffers for their sins before their very eyes through the magic of film.

Gibson has given the Catholic Church what it wanted and perhaps needed: an occasion to embrace its own fundamentalism. Certainly the Church has neither rejected nor distanced itself from *The Passion*. Priests took whole congregations to see it on Easter Sunday, and viewing the film may well become an annual ritual in the tradition of Passion plays.

Set aside the question of personal lenses and one is still left with the concern that Gibson's film marks the unofficial return to the pre–Vatican II catechesis of Church doctrine. In following the literal words of the Gospel it reasserts the dogma that the Vatican in its ecumenical moments has qualified, but a dogma that can be traced back to the earliest days of Catholicism: *extra ecclesiam nulla salus*—outside the Church there is no salvation, no way to God the Father except through his son Jesus. And it vividly recreates the images of the stiff-necked Jews who instead of embracing salvation pronounced a sentence of death against their own Messiah.

Gibson has been faithful to his own radical form of Catholicism, which rejects Vatican II, with its affirmation of religious toleration. His *Passion* gives us that traditional faith without the spirit of ecumenical respect for Judaism, Islam, and other religions to which the Church pledged itself in Vatican II. It was a pledge that left open the possibility of salvation outside the Church and of forgiveness for everyone made in God's image. If Vatican II was in large measure a response to the Holocaust and to the Church's own history of anti-Semitism, then the success of *The Passion* is a cultural event that signals the end of that Christian feeling of remorse. If it does nothing else, *The Passion* should remind us all that the impulse of fundamentalism now sweeping the world is dividing humanity even as it seeks a more sacred community.

For God and Country

Henry V, 1944, 1989

LEGEND HAS IT THAT WINSTON CHURCHILL asked Laurence Olivier to make a film version of Shakespeare's *Henry V* to help raise British morale during the worst days of World War II. It was not an entirely original idea. The British have had a tradition of throwing *Henry V* "once more unto the breach" to rally the citizenry for war. By the 19th century the play had been transformed into a spectacle of patriotic pageantry celebrating imperial Britain. By the turn of the 20th century and the Boer War, Shakespeare's Henry was back on the traditional stage, but with flags waving and raucous London audiences standing to cheer the great St. Crispin's Day speech. During World War I, as Britain suffered through the horrible sacrifice of its young men in the muddy trenches of France, an invincible Henry V reminded audiences that God was on their side.

Olivier accomplished everything that Churchill asked of him and more. Working with all the resources that wartime England could provide, including one of the first good Technicolor cameras, Olivier made the most inspiring Henry V and the greatest Shakespeare film of his time.

Olivier's 1944 film had its American premiere in 1946. James Agee, reviewing it for *Time*, was unstinting in his praise: "Sometimes ... it improves on the original. Yet its brilliance is graceful, never self-assertive. It simply subserves, extends, illuminates and liberates Shakespeare's poem." Olivier's *Henry V* had helped the Allied war effort and made Shakespeare accessible to the masses. The Allies had just defeated an axis of evil, and no one questioned that God was on their side, the atrocities on the others', or doubted the justice of the cause, or begrudged the sainted glory of their leaders. Olivier confirmed the people's faith and proved the old Ukrainian proverb, "When the banner is unfurled, all reason is in the trumpet." Hollywood basked in Olivier's reflected glory and awarded him an honorary Oscar in 1946 for his work on the film.

But Shakespeare scholars noted that the original play was interlaced with lines that cut against Olivier's theme of martial glory and royal heroism. Like his banner-waving 19th-century predecessors, Olivier had performed drastic cosmetic surgery on Shakespeare's "poem."

To appreciate Olivier's makeover one has to read the play with care and then watch the refurbished video. Anything in the text that might diminish the glory of Henry V or the justice of his war has been bent to Olivier's purpose or simply excised. The pivotal consideration of the play—whether Henry V had a just cause for going to war or whether, as William Hazlitt wrote in 1817, he had simply been given carte blanche by the "pious and politic Archbishop of Canterbury ... to rob and murder in circles of latitude and longitude abroad—to save the possessions of the church at home"—has been turned into brief, farcical stage business. The original first scene of the play has the Archbishop of Canterbury worrying to his sycophant, the Bishop of Ely, that the new king and his parliament are reconsidering the passage of a law urged during his father's reign. The law would take back for the king all the wealth left by the devout to the Church. To avoid this financial disaster the archbishop points the young king toward France, where there is far more wealth than the Church of England can provide. The archbishop expounds on the law and the Bible to assure the king that he has a legal claim to the throne of France. Such is the casus belli of Henry V's chapter in the Hundred Years' War.

Olivier edits out the offending lines and makes the warmongering episcopates into laughable fools. Gone completely, too, are the lines at the siege of Harfleur where Henry threatens the French governor with atrocities if he fails to surrender: "The gates of mercy shall be all shut up"; "look to see / The blind and bloody soldier with foul hand / Defile the locks of your shrill-shrieking daughters; / Your fathers taken by the silver beards, / And their most reverend heads dash'd to the walls, / Your naked infants spitted upon pikes." The speech threatens mass rape of Harfleur's women three times. Omitted, too, are the disturbing lines during the Battle of Agincourt when Henry orders, "Every soldier kill his prisoners." Olivier's saintly Henry is an unspotted king who reacts instead to French atrocity only thus: "I was not angry since I came to France / Until this instant." So the audience will share his righteous anger, Olivier has the French act first, attacking the boys and the luggage. He presents this episode as led by the cowardly French dauphin, who thus becomes the embodiment of the evil enemy. The list of omissions goes on, but the most striking is Shakespeare's epilogue, which speaks to the futility of the war: "They lost France and made his England bleed."

Dame Judi Dench quoted this epilogue when asked to judge a May 2004 debate—between Christopher Hitchens, David Brooks, Christopher Buckley, Arianna Huffington, and Ken Adelman, among others—about the merits of George W. Bush's invasion of Iraq informed by competing interpretations of *Henry V*. Organized as a fundraiser for the Washington, D.C., Shakespeare Theatre, the debate seems to have been a friendly pre-election joust between Republican hawks and Democratic doves, with the hawks relying on some version of Olivier's sanctimonious interpretation. Dame Judi Dench, herself a Quaker, refused to declare a winner. As it happened, she had appeared as Mistress Quickly in Kenneth Branagh's darker, post-Falklands movie version of the play, released in 1989. (She speaks the famous lines describing Falstaff's death and blaming the king for breaking his heart.) Branagh shows us much of what Olivier did not—that there can be a mix of good and evil on both sides and that innocent people bear the greatest burden of suffering. Viewed side by side with Olivier's version, Branagh's is the obvious winner, with time, history, and the text all on his side.

BRANAGH'S HENRY V IS A FAR SUPERIOR film and a more sophisticated reading of Shakespeare, but it must have taken a self-confidence bordering on arrogance for a young actor to attempt to match Sir Laurence's monumental achievement. Branagh explores the psychological dimensions of the character—his transformation from the wild young man whom Falstaff loved to the King who repudiates his tavern friend ("I know thee not, old man") and grows into his royal responsibilities. Whereas

Olivier orates in his first scenes, Branagh converses. His episcopates are not fools, but with shortened lines they are not as conniving as their entire speeches might reveal. Branagh's young King Henry clearly relies on their advice. The film includes scenes that emphasize the king's break with his past—for example, the execution of three traitors, one of them a lord who shared "his bed"—and he ratifies the hanging of Bardolph (one of Falstaff's lower-class tavern fraternity) for stealing from a French church. On the night before the Battle of Agincourt, as the king prays, he expresses his fear that God may not recognize his father's claim, and thus his own, to the English throne. In Branagh's St. Crispin's Day speech, less exquisite than Olivier's but more compelling, he tries to lift himself up as well as his men. His character has to earn the kingly glory with which Olivier begins the play. Branagh's battle is fought in a muddy field on a rainy day where arrows strike their victims and blood is spilled.

The iconic war scene has Henry carrying in his arms the dead body of one of the boys killed by the French, and in the end his chorus, Derek Jacobi, delivers the epilogue of futility. But Branagh's Henry V, though more psychological and darker, does not break with the tradition that portrays this Henry as the "star of England" and Shakespeare's greatest king.

It was a tradition criticized from the time of Hazlitt: "Henry, because he did not know how to govern his own kingdom, determined to make war upon his neighbours." In Shakespeare's text, Henry IV, speaking from his deathbed, urges this strategy on his son. It is not always clear whether Hazlitt was describing Shakespeare's Henry V or the historical king. But there can be no mistaking Stephen Greenblatt's 1988 characterization: "The play deftly registers every nuance of royal hypocrisy, ruthlessness, and bad faith—testing, in effect, the proposition that successful rule depends not upon sacredness but upon demonic violence—but it does so in the context of a celebration." One can almost sense T.W. Craik, the editor of the Arden edition of the play, cringing as he dutifully cited Greenblatt's "new historicist" reading of the play—a reading he rejects with every fiber of his loyal British soul. He blames Hazlitt for initiating the critical political readings of the play, which find so much irony in it.

Irony is a magic wand of literary interpretation that can turn words of love into hate, good into evil, and truth into falsehood. One is, as Harold Bloom suggests, free to surmise how much Shakespeare himself provided in these two "patriotic romps." But as the recent history of *Henry V* productions suggests, such judgments of irony depend on directors' political opinions about contemporary wars. An American production of the play during the Vietnam War made Henry V an ignoble Lyndon Johnson destroying the vineyards of France in order to save them. After the invasion of

Iraq, Nicholas Hytner, in his first production as director of the National Theatre in London, reinvented Henry V as Tony Blair, a handsome, honey-tongued politician complicit in a war of colonization and trying to justify it. Staged in modern dress and stripping away the patriotic fervor, Hytner's production emphasized the human cost of war. The king's speeches were presented as press conferences, and the chorus was Henry V's spin doctors broadcasting on large television sets mounted around the stage.

Here in the United States it is George W. Bush who is compared to Henry V, despite the president's limitations as a speaker. The parallels between the king and our president are intriguing and even disturbing. Both leaders are hard-drinking playboys who found God, mended their ways, and followed their fathers into office. Both men's claims to that office were sullied—Henry V's by the murder of Richard II and George W. Bush's by the Supreme Court's intervention. Both men were heavily reliant on their fathers' more-experienced advisers. Henry's self-interested church advisers, dubbed "theocons" by David Brooks in the Shakespeare Theatre debate, seem not unlike those who told George W. Bush about the weapons of mass destruction that would be found in Iraq. Both teams of advisers assured their leaders that they could win their wars using much less than the full measure of their available military force. And both teams promised easy victories and long-term benefits. Out of Henry V's conquest of France would come Joan of Arc and a war of resistance that for the first time would unify France as a nation. Out of George W. Bush's conquest of Iraq has come a Sunni insurgency and an energized Islam with new leaders treated as saints.

One might take all this as far-fetched historical coincidence, of interest only to bardolators. There is, however, a deeper and more frightening resonance between Harfleur and Fallujah and between Henry V and George W.

Bush. The Shakespeare scholar Herschel Baker noted that in *Henry V* patriotism is presented as an aspect of religion, and the same frightening conjunction is made by George W. Bush and his own theocon advisers. To be against George W. Bush and his Iraq war is to be against God and country, a heathen and a traitor.

I cannot claim that Shakespeare had this issue of patriotism and religion in mind when he wrote *Henry V*. But I do think that his play has a particular importance for our times and our America. Yes, Shakespeare's text is filled with contradictions—contradictions that Olivier cut out and that Branagh used to explore the psychological development of the young king. Harold Bloom is doubtless correct that both films ignore the blatant hypocrisy and bad faith and send the audience away feeling nostalgic for the glory of imperial England. Directors like Hytner work the textual contradictions and, wielding the magic wand of irony, lead their audiences to the opposite moral conclusion. The critic Norman Rabkin suggests that in *Henry V*, "Shakespeare creates a work whose ultimate power is precisely the fact that it points in two opposite directions, virtually daring us to choose one of the two opposed interpretations it requires of us." T.W. Craik, who quotes Rabkin, doubts that "a spectator can preserve this state of moral suspension and still receive satisfaction."

Yet much of Shakespeare, including the sonnets, has this quality: there is thesis and antithesis but no synthesis. When common sense demands the satisfaction of a conclusion, the sonnets become banal. I want to disagree with Rabkin—I think Shakespeare is daring us not to choose. And I hope Craik is wrong and that a state of moral suspension can be deeply satisfying to Shakespeare's audience in the 21st century. For it is precisely the refusal to yield to easy moral conclusions that makes Shakespeare's work in general and the text of *Henry V* in particular relevant for our times.

A Forbidden Hope

Water, 2005

IN FEBRUARY 2000 DEEPA MEHTA HAD built her sets and begun filming on the ghats that run along the Ganges River in India's holy city of Varanasi (Benares). The location was critical to her story of a widows' ashram on the banks of the river where 14 women live in penury and constant prayer, condemned by their husbands' deaths and shunned by ordinary people as omens of bad luck. With white saris and shaved heads, sick and elderly widows traditionally come from all across India to Varanasi in the belief that if they die in the holy city and their ashes are spread on the sacred waters of the river they will find salvation. A decade earlier Mehta had seen such a widow: a skeleton-thin old lady on her hands and knees, blindly searching for her lost spectacles while the passing pilgrims avoided her. Mehta's unshakable memory of that widow, "bent over like a shrimp," would eventually inspire the screenplay for *Water*. Following her films *Fire* in 1996 and *Earth* in 1998, it was to complete what she called her Elemental Trilogy.

Mehta set the film in 1938 during the rise of Gandhi. Although by then the infamous tradition of suttee—the burning of women on their husbands' funeral pyres—had long since been abandoned, widows were still required under Hindu religious law to retreat from the world and live a life of mourning and penitence. According to Hindu belief, the sins of women in their past lives had caused the deaths of their husbands. The harsh consequences of these beliefs were compounded by the practice of arranged marriages, in which young girls could be given as brides to old and even dying husbands. Mehta's ashram on the Ganges includes an eight-year-old widow, destined to live her entire life in severe discipline—while the obese old matriarch who rules the ashram supports her appetite for forbidden sweets and bhang (a form of hashish) by selling the services of a beautiful widow to rich Brahmin men on the other side of the river.

Mehta has said that the Indian Ministry of Information and Broadcasting—which censors and approves screenplays before they can be shot—granted her all the necessary permits. But Hindu fundamentalists, who had been fulminating about Mehta's sacrilegious treatment of holy scriptures ever since *Fire*, torched the sets, threw them into the Ganges, and burned Mehta in effigy. When *Fire* was released in India, they had thrown Molotov cocktails at the screen and closed down theaters. This time they preemptively threatened to riot if Mehta began filming. The local authorities of Uttar Pradesh were unable to guarantee adequate protection, and Mehta had to look for alternative sites. It took her four years to find a substitute for Varanasi, but beside the still waters of Bolgoda Lake in Sri Lanka, Mehta created a timeless Varanasi of the imagination.

The set design is one of the many stunning accomplishments of the film; every shot of Giles Nuttgen's cinematography is a work of art, and there are moments of serene beauty. Indeed, *Water* is far and away Mehta's greatest achievement and deserves to be compared with the masterwork of Indian cinema, the Apu trilogy of Satyajit Ray.

Mehta's earlier films, and particularly those in the Elemental Trilogy, would not have led one to expect the deep humanism, epic power, technical mastery, and sheer beauty of *Water*. With this film Mehta has turned all her weaknesses into strengths. The psychological themes she has worked and reworked—as though she were settling a personal score—become here an expansive portrayal of the human condition. Her stock storytelling device—in which everything is seen through the eyes of an innocent—takes on narrative force through the rebellious eight-year-old child, Chuyia, who refuses to accept her fate. Mehta's earlier attempts to create epic scenes lacked verisimilitude; in *Water* the reenactment of Gandhi's visit to a thronged train station is totally convincing. And Mehta's own ironic and condescending attitudes toward Hindu traditions are here mediated by characters struggling with their faith.

Mehta was born into a well-to-do Hindu family in India. Her own widowed grandmother, she says, far from being an outcast, was a tyrannical matriarch. Mehta's father was a film distributor and theater owner, and Mehta spent many afternoons with her friends watching films. The family was ambitious: her older brother Dilip was an internationally renowned still photographer by the time he was 24, and Mehta set her own sights on becoming a philosopher—a more common route to filmmaking these days than one might suppose. Like many graduate students, Mehta could not settle on a Ph.D. thesis topic, and when someone at a dinner party offered her a job as a gofer in a documentary-film studio she jumped at the opportunity. She started honing her film-making skills and made her first documentary about the arranged marriage of a 15-year-old girl, an untouchable, who cleaned the floors in the Mehtas' own home.

She married the Canadian filmmaker Paul Saltzman and immigrated to Toronto. The couple started making documentaries together, one about her brother Dilip, who often worked with them. In her first feature film, released in 1991, she acknowledges exploring psychological and cultural issues that were important in her life. The film, *Sam and Me*, was about a young Muslim Indian who has immigrated to Toronto and gets a job taking care of an old Jew, Sam Cohen. Sam is no longer interested in life and wants only to be buried in Israel. His family does not really want to bother with him. But something unexpected happens: the young Muslim and the old Jew discover that they enjoy each other's company. Their friendship upsets both families, who interfere with unhappy consequences.

The success of *Sam and Me* brought Mehta to the attention of George Lucas, who hired her to make two episodes of the television series *The Young Indiana Jones Chronicles*, one of them set in Varanasi, circa 1910. It was during the filming of that episode that she saw the unforgettable image of the old widow. And it was during that production that she worked for the first time with Giles Nuttgens, the talented cinematographer who would film the entire Elemental Trilogy.

Mehta's career was launched, but her marriage disintegrated. During the months leading up to her divorce she threw herself into writing *Fire*, set in modern-day India. Returning to India to film, she was not the prodigal child asking forgiveness and embracing the traditions that still require women's subservience. Her Elemental Trilogy was to be a challenge to the chauvinism of Hindu orthodoxy.

Fire is a story of sexual hypocrisy in a lower-middle-class Hindu family in Delhi. The family—an elderly mother disabled by a stroke, her two sons, their wives, and a male servant—live together above their takeout restaurant and video store. The wives are unloved and sexually rejected by their husbands; the male servant is repulsive in his own way. The older brother prides himself on living a life of pious abstinence, *brahmacharin*, based on the Hindu belief that desire is the root cause of rebirth into the cycle of suffering. In reality he is punishing his wife, whom he blames because they have been unable to have children. She accepts the blame and works hard to take care of the family and the restaurant. Having established the sordid nature of the men of the family, Mehta draws the victimized wives into a lesbian love affair. Mehta affirms this sexual relationship.

Rebelling against her servitude, the elder of the two wives tells her pious husband that she has chosen to live a life instead of penitently waiting for death.

What had fundamentalists firebombing movie screens was that in addition to mocking religious asceticism and affirming lesbianism, Mehta's screenplay parodied a famous story in Hindu scripture. Sita, the goddess, proves that she has been sexually faithful to her husband, the god Rama, by going through a trial by fire; nonetheless, she is exiled. Mehta's heroine, the older sister-in-law, is subjected to an enactment of the trial by fire when her husband discovers her lesbian affair. She survives the fire but abandons her husband and leaves home to rendezvous with her lover. The controversy surrounding *Fire* had a longer life than the film itself and made Mehta's reputation.

Earth, the next film in the trilogy, was based on Bapsi Sidhwa's best-selling novel *Cracking India*. It described, from a child's point of view, the tumultuous year of 1947, when India was partitioned and millions of Muslims, Hindus, and Sikhs were turned out of their homes and slaughtered by their neighbors. Unfortunately, neither the acting nor the epic scenes were compelling enough to make the novel come to life on the screen.

Water could have easily been much like *Earth*. She was preparing to use many of the same actors and many of the same themes. But when the fundamentalists forced her to temporarily set that film aside, she turned her attention to a lighter film that may in the end have brought new life to the trilogy. That film was *Bollywood/Hollywood*, a thoroughly entertaining musical comedy that became a huge commercial success in Canada and elsewhere in the Indian diaspora. It playfully engages the conflicts of Indian identity and assimilation, conflicts that Mehta still struggles with herself, and gives them a comic resolution in which love conquers all.

For *Bollywood/Hollywood* she needed a glamorous leading actress, and she cast Lisa Ray, a woman of Indian and Polish descent who has become India's foremost fashion model. When Mehta returned to *Water* she brought Ray with her to play Kalyani, the beautiful widow who is sold into prostitution. There is a love story in *Water*: Narayan, a young lawyer from a wealthy Brahmin family, sees Kalyani in the street, and it is love at first sight—a love that transgresses the taboo against widows and the caste system. Mehta gave the part of Narayan to a Bollywood star and India's most celebrated male model, John Abraham, a man who had appeared on the cover of as many magazines as Lisa Ray. Although he plays the role of a recent law-school graduate circa 1938, he appears in the film sporting the kind of three-day beard that currently seems required of young male actors. That said, Ray and Abraham give winning performances that do credit to Mehta. Kalyani is a simple, uneducated woman, the lotus that preserves its innocence even as it floats in corruption. Within those parameters Ray is superb. Narayan is a Gandhian idealist who has to convince us that he truly feels love and is not just a fool—and he succeeds.

More daring was Mehta's selection of the actress to play Chuyia, the feisty girl who will challenge the traditions of the ashram. When the film begins we see the child sucking on a stalk of sugar cane and riding on the back of a wagon through the countryside. A man is stretched out on the wagon bed, and she cheekily pokes his feet; only later will we realize that he is the child's dying husband. The marriage seems never to have been consummated, and there has been no wedding, but this little girl is about to become a widow. Her parents piously abandon her in the ashram, and her head is shaved in a ritual of degradation. Since Mehta would be filming in Sri Lanka, she began searching there for a child to play Chuyia. The girl she discovered, Sarala, did not speak

Hindi and had to learn all her lines by rote. But she is a spirited presence who speaks the lines that one imagines are closest to Mehta's heart: "Where are all the male widows?"

Mehta's ashram is peopled with crones out of Fellini movies, and their ensemble acting is superb. Madhumati, the obese matriarch of the ashram who exploits Kalyani to satisfy her appetites, is still shown to us in all her humanity—a tribute to Mehta's and the actress's talent. But it is the widow Shakuntala, played by the great Indian actress Seema Biswas—known to Western audiences for her role as Phoolan Devi in Shekhar Kapur's *Bandit Queen*—whose performance holds the film together. Shakuntala is the conscience and quiet strength of the ashram. She is the one who mediates the struggle between deep religious faith and the truth as she sees and understands it. And she struggles to resolve this not out of self-interest—she accepts her own fate—but out of her concern for Chuyia and Kalyani.

When, despite the religious taboos and his parents' high social position, Narayan resolves to marry the beautiful illiterate widow, tragedy ensues. He is escorting her to his home across the river when she recognizes the way: she has been his father's prostitute. She insists on turning back and later drowns herself in the river where she has so often cleansed her body and her soul. And this is not the worst that can happen in Mehta's tragic imagination. The obese crone, not to be denied her luxuries, sends the innocent Chuyia across the river to the rich Brahmins. The horrified Shakuntala is waiting at the dock when the feisty child, now devastated, is returned the next morning. She takes the child in her arms to the railroad station where Gandhi is making a brief stop. If there is hope in this corrupted world, she finds it in Gandhi, not the religious tradition she has followed. With Chuyia in her arms she listens with the throngs of people to Gandhi's message. He reenters the train, and it slowly begins to leave the station. Shakuntala now knows what to do: chasing the train with the child in her arms, she spots Narayan, who is leaving with Gandhi. Desperately, she hands the ruined child over to his care.

Preposterous, yes! Melodramatic, yes! But in this it is like many great movies. There was not a dry eye in the audience as that train moved into the distance. Mehta has proved in *Water* that she is more than an angry iconoclast. In the darker passages of the moral adventure of life, films like *Water* allow us to hope.

BOSTON REVIEW BOOKS

Boston Review Books are accessible, short books that take ideas seriously. They are animated by hope, committed to equality, and convinced that the imagination eludes political categories. The editors aim to establish a public space in which people can loosen the hold of conventional preconceptions and start to reason together across the lines others are so busily drawing.